LEADING THE SHIFT

Enhancing Operational Efficiency With AI

by
Chris Loveday

Grosvenor House
Publishing Limited

"Chris Loveday is a pioneer with deep practical experience of AI across education, especially back office. This book is a must read."

Sir Anthony Seldon
Educator and Author

"The definition of insanity is doing the same thing and expecting a better outcome. As a pioneering school business professional, Chris Loveday shows us that by thinking differently and being brave with the application of technology, we can find a new way and a better way. If you're serious about improving your approach to operations and want to enjoy the associated capacity gains, this is a must-read."

Stephen Morales
Chief Executive Officer, Institute of School Business Leadership

"An inspiring and accessible guide, this book is essential reading—a masterclass in navigating change and driving digital transformation with confidence and vision."

Julia Adamson MBE
Education Director, BCS, The Chartered Institute for IT

"*Leading the Shift* turns AI from a buzzword into a practical, ethically grounded playbook for colleges. Loveday blends hands-on experience with a deep understanding of culture and safeguarding, producing the first guide I'm happy to hand to any leader who asks how to make AI work—safely and at scale—in real educational settings."

David Foster
Founding Partner, ADSP and Author

"A refreshingly honest guide that demonstrates how AI can transform educational operations—not just classrooms. The author's methodical approach provides invaluable guidance for any institution embarking on their AI journey."

Professor Rose Luckin
University College London, Founder educateventures.com,
Author and Speaker

"This isn't about the latest tech trend or adding more to your plate, it's a very down-to-earth, practical guide on how AI can actually help schools and colleges run more efficiently. It's packed with real experiences, not just theory, showing how AI can, where appropriate, reduce admin, ease pressure on staff, and give back valuable time to focus on what really matters.

The chapters are all broken down and signposted section by section so you can dip in and out of the book identifying specific topics as needed. It's clear, honest and packed with ideas you can use right away. I recommend it for anyone in education who's curious about using technology in a way that's thoughtful, purposeful and genuinely helpful."

Al Kingsley MBE
Multi Academy Trust Chair, EdTech CEO and Author

"Chris Loveday has first-hand and front-line experience of delivering practical applications in AI in a college, and this shows in his excellent publication. This is a treasure trove of examples of AI in action, and it addresses head-on the pitfalls and benefits of introducing a rich variety of AI-supported developments.

This publication helpfully encourages the reader to view AI through a lens of positive opportunity, rather than one of anxiety – about plagiarism in assessment, for example – that has been a feature of much of the earlier dialogue.

But this is also a pragmatic resource and does not shy away from addressing the real difficulties and challenges associated with implementing new ideas and identifying new opportunities, which confront organisations that are dealing with such a transformational development changing at astonishing speed."

Bill Watkin CBE
CEO, Sixth Form College Association

"Many organisational leaders are aware that AI will revolutionise the sectors and environments they operate in. They know their organisations need to embrace it, but they do not have the slightest idea how to start this process. This book will help them. Although positioned in the setting of an educational institution, this work has relevance for all leaders.

Its core messages and questions provide critical insights. AI adoption is not primarily a technical issue. It is a people issue. What type of organisation do you want to be? How will AI help you achieve this? How will you integrate AI in your human ecosystem in a people-centric way? How should the change be handled? How can you ensure employees embrace AI rather than fear and resist it?"

Geoff Glover
Academic Tutor (Southampton Solent University),
Founder and Steering Committee Member of TechSolent

"Many of us are still experimenting with prompts and platforms, but Chris is doing something different. He's pioneering.

Leading the Shift offers a clear, grounded roadmap for using AI to improve operational efficiency in schools and colleges. Rather than chasing trends, Loveday focuses on real challenges: reducing staff workload, improving systems, and delivering better outcomes for students and staff alike.

From in-house agent development to building digital trust and capability, it's packed with insights from lived experience. It's not about chasing trends. It's about action.

Chris isn't just using AI. He's helping build the future of how education works, and this book gives you the tools to start doing the same."

Matthew Wemyss
Educator and Author

"*Leading the Shift* cuts through the AI hype and delivers a practical, insightful guide for leaders. Filled with real-world experience and actionable strategies this book is essential for anyone looking to implement AI solutions that truly make a difference."

Dr Jamie Smith
Entrepreneur, Advisor and Speaker

All rights reserved
Copyright © Chris Loveday, 2025

The right of Chris Loveday to be identified as the author of this work has been asserted in accordance with Section 78 of the Copyright, Designs and Patents Act 1988

The book cover is copyright to Chris Loveday

This book is published by
Grosvenor House Publishing Ltd
Link House
140 The Broadway, Tolworth, Surrey, KT6 7HT.
www.grosvenorhousepublishing.co.uk

This book is sold subject to the conditions that it shall not, by way of trade or otherwise, be lent, resold, hired out or otherwise circulated without the author's or publisher's prior consent in any form of binding or cover other than that in which it is published and without a similar condition including this condition being imposed on the subsequent purchaser.

A CIP record for this book
is available from the British Library

Paperback ISBN 978-1-83615-321-4
Hardback ISBN 978-1-83615-322-1
eBook ISBN 978-1-83615-323-8

CONTENT

Welcome	xi
Foreword	xiii
Executive Summary	xv
Introduction	xvii
Chapter 1: Why AI, Why Now?	1
Seeing the Opportunity: Visionary Leadership and Strategic Insight	3
Building from a Solid Foundation	5
From Curiosity to Commitment	7
Seeking the Right Expertise	9
Intent Over Impulse: Leading with Purpose, Not Hype	12
Conclusion: Purpose, Not Panic	14
Chapter 1: 🧠 What We Learned	15
Chapter 1: 💡 Key Reflection Questions	15
Chapter 2: Laying the Groundwork	16
Mapping the Landscape	17
Bringing in External Experts	19
Early Strategic Choices	22
Building a Culture of AI Readiness	30
From Foundations to First Builds	32
Leading by Example: A Strategic Investment in Premium Education Licenses	33
Conclusion: Culture Before Code	35
Chapter 2: 🧠 What We Learned	36
Chapter 2: 💡 Key Reflection Questions	36
Chapter 3: Building AI from the Inside Out	37
Understanding APIs: A Gateway to Bespoke AI Agents	39
Our Initial Flagship Agents	41

Back Office Agents: AI Agents That Transformed Our Operational Efficiency	46
The Broader Agent Development and Ecosystem	50
Inside-Out Innovation: The Strategic Advantages of Building Our Own AI Solutions	52
Conclusion: Building with Purpose, Scaling with Confidence	55
Chapter 3: 🧠 What We Learned	56
Chapter 3: 💡 Key Reflection Questions	56

Chapter 4: Overcoming Challenges and Managing Risks — 57

Navigating the Complexity of Early Adoption	58
Agreeing Priorities and Defining Outcomes	60
Managing the Cost of Innovation	61
Managing Expectations and Avoiding the Hype	63
Ethical, Technical, and Cultural Risks	65
Understanding AI Hallucinations and Their Value in the Right Situations	69
Practical Implementation Barriers	71
Digital Equity: Bridging the Divide in a Rapidly Advancing World	73
Conclusion: Courage, Clarity and the Willingness to Learn	75
Chapter 4: 🧠 What We Learned	77
Chapter 4: 💡 Key Reflection Questions	77

Chapter 5: Unlocking the Benefits of AI in Education — 78

From Efficiency to Empowerment	79
Enhancing Staff Capability and Confidence	80
Elevating the Student Experience	82
A Culture of Continuous Improvement	84
Embedding Inclusion and Ethical Practice	86
Strategic Alignment and Organisational Learning	87
Conclusion: The Real Benefit? A Culture of Possibility	89
Chapter 5: 🧠 What We Learned	91
Chapter 5: 💡 Key Reflection Questions	91

Chapter 6: Leading a Cultural Shift	92
From Compliance to Curiosity	93
Redefining Professional Identity	94
Leadership as Culture-Making	96
From Users to Co-Creators	98
Embedding Language and Values	100
Making it Stick	102
Conclusion: Culture as Capability	105
Chapter 6: 🧠 What We Learned	107
Chapter 6: 💡 Key Reflection Questions	107
Chapter 7: Scaling for the Future	108
Building on a Strong, Localised Core	109
From Agents to Ecosystems	111
Scaling Without Losing Trust	113
Capacity as a Strategic Asset	116
Scaling Through Partnerships	118
The Future: Scaling with Purpose	120
Conclusion: Scaling as a Way of Thinking	123
Chapter 7: 🧠 What We Learned	125
Chapter 7: 💡 Key Reflection Questions	125
Chapter 8: Lessons Learned and Guidance for Education Leaders	126
Establish an AI Policy, No Matter Where You Stand	127
Lead with Strategy, Not Hype	129
Start Small, Think Big	131
Own the Build Where You Can	132
Focus on People, Not Just Products	134
Design for Inclusion and Ethics from Day One	136
Think in Systems, Not Silos	138
Capacity Building Is Key to Sustainability	140
Open Your Doors, And Your Thinking	142
Keep Asking the Right Questions	144
Don't Wait for Certainty, Lead with Courage	146
Legal Compliance: Navigating the Regulatory Landscape	148

Final Thoughts: Leading with Intention, Building with Integrity	151
Chapter 8: 💬 What We Learned	152
Chapter 8: 💡 Key Reflection Questions	153
Chapter 9: Enough About Me, What About You?	154
AI Agent Design Canvas	154
AI Readiness Self-Audit (for SLTs)	156
Anatomy of an AI Project Budget	157
3 Month Action Plan: A Starting Roadmap	158
Leadership Skills and CPD Reflection Tool	159
Chapter 9: 💬 What We Learned	160
Chapter 9: 💡 Key Reflection Questions	161
Bonus Chapter: Operational Excellence and the ISBL Framework	162
Key Terms and Definitions	166
Acknowledgements	170
References	172

WELCOME

Welcome, and thank you for picking up this book, a reflection of my journey, passions, and commitment to driving meaningful change in education.

I'm Chris Loveday, my current role is that of a Vice Principal in the post 16 education sector. Although my career in education spans over two decades, beginning in the secondary school sector where I dedicated 21 years, 10 of which were in school leadership and business management, before moving into the dynamic world of post 16 education. I am passionate about social mobility, EdTech, and artificial intelligence.

Over the past 15 months, I have led a project of strategic and operational transformation through artificial intelligence.

Beyond my current role, I have been working with the Chiltern Learning Trust on the Department for Education (DfE) AI resources for teachers and leaders. I contribute nationally as a member of the AI in Education Strategic Committee and Chair of the CFO/COO Panel. I have had the pleasure of presenting at conferences up and down the country on our journey with AI.

But perhaps most importantly, I'm also a proud father of two wonderful sons and a loving husband. My family gives me the motivation and grounding to strive for a better future, both at home and in the education system. Balancing family life with a professional career and academic advancement is not without its challenges, especially as I currently study for a double master's: an MBA and a Master's in Strategic Leadership. This ongoing personal development fuels my belief in lifelong learning and equips me with the tools to lead with clarity, purpose and empathy.

I've written this book for fellow leaders, school business professionals, and education changemakers who are ready to harness the potential of AI to boost operational efficiency and deliver greater value to our communities. Whether you're just beginning your journey or already deep in transformation, I hope this book provides you with inspiration, practical insights, and a renewed sense of purpose.

Thank you for joining me. Let's shape the future of education together.

Chris Loveday

FOREWORD

For many years, we've seen school operations management as a necessary distraction from the business of teaching and learning, but all too often not as a core integrated leadership activity. It is for this reason that leadership is sometimes disjointed[1] and operates in silos. With pedagogical leaders focusing on school improvement and school business leaders doing finance and HR, technology and infrastructure are afterthoughts that often don't have a natural home. Chris Loveday, through this book, shows us how to work and think differently. He offers solutions that provide an opportunity to unleash greater potential if we are prepared to embrace innovation and lean into the expertise of professionals from different backgrounds and with unique technical expertise.

Using Operational Excellence (OpEx) methodology (described in the Bonus Chapter) combined with Digital Innovation (DI), our education sector can unlock substantial capacity gains for a system desperately in need of operational and leadership bandwidth.

At its core, Operational Excellence is about doing business better, by continuously improving processes, reducing waste, increasing efficiency, and aligning everyone to customer value. For the avoidance of doubt, a customer is anyone in receipt of a service.

OpEx aims to yield faster throughput, fewer errors, less rework and duplication, better resource utilisation, and shorter lead times.

---

1 Morales, S. (2022). Barriers to joined-up leadership.

DI supports OpEx through increased automation (robotic process automation, AI, machine learning), better data analytics, and the power of human augmentation.

Together, DI and OpEx improve visibility, decision-making, and scalability by providing critical information in real time, removing unnecessary manual effort, ensuring seamless workflow efficiency, enhancing collaboration, and eliminating errors.

For those prepared to embrace the thinking contained within this book, the size of the prize is enormous. I would go further: failure to innovate is a failure to improve, and the ultimate losers of those not prepared to adopt new/better approaches to operations management are the nation's children.

Stephen Morales
Chief Executive Officer, Institute of School Business Leadership

EXECUTIVE SUMMARY

Leading the Shift: Enhancing Operational Efficiency With AI offers a grounded, experience-led guide to embedding artificial intelligence (AI) into the operational core of educational institutions. Drawing directly on the strategic and cultural transformation led at a Sixth Form College, the book presents a practical blueprint for leaders who are ready to explore the role of AI beyond the classroom, where the most immediate impact can be made.

Rather than focusing on futuristic visions or classroom disruption, this book reframes AI as a tool for resolving today's pressing operational challenges: administrative inefficiencies, rising staff workloads, siloed digital systems, and constrained resources. It demonstrates how AI, when implemented with intention and aligned to organisational values, can significantly enhance capacity, accuracy, and service delivery across support functions.

The narrative is built around a real-world implementation journey, from early strategic visioning and cultural groundwork, through agent development and system integration, to the scaling of bespoke AI solutions. At every stage, the emphasis is on ethical deployment, sustainable change, and inclusive leadership.

Key themes include:

- Strategic Leadership and Change Models: Applying frameworks such as Burke-Litwin, Kotter, ADKAR, and the Technology Acceptance Model to align AI implementation with organisational purpose and strategic goals.

- In-House Innovation: Building custom AI agents within the institution's digital tenancy to maintain control, ensure compliance, and maximise relevance, avoiding reliance on costly, inflexible commercial tools.
- Culture as Catalyst: Prioritising people, not platforms. Establishing digital trust, psychological safety, and staff engagement as foundations for sustainable transformation.
- Evidence-Led Impact: Documenting measurable benefits, from hundreds of hours saved in administrative processes to improved staff experience and digital maturity.
- Scalable Systems, Not Shiny Solutions: Shifting from tool-led to system-led thinking, with a focus on interoperability, governance, and long-term adaptability.

This book is not a technical manual or a theoretical manifesto. It is a leadership guide written from inside the process of change. Designed for school business leaders, senior leadership teams, governors, and policymakers, it offers both strategic insight and operational tools, including reflection questions, audit templates, and case studies.

Above all, *Leading the Shift* challenges education leaders to stop waiting for perfect conditions, and instead lead with courage, clarity, and care, shaping the future of education one intentional decision at a time.

INTRODUCTION

This book is for leaders working in settings who are ready to explore how artificial intelligence (AI) can drive operational effectiveness and efficiency. Whether you are a school business manager, a headteacher, a senior leader in a college, university or multi-academy trust, this guide will help you navigate the practical side of AI implementation, not the hype, but the reality.

While the headlines have been dominated by bold promises, AI as the "personal tutor in every child's pocket," or the idea that automation will soon replace entire swathes of the curriculum, we took a different approach. Whilst our journey with AI focused on the here and now. We looked at the everyday operational challenges that leaders face: managing limited budgets, streamlining administrative tasks, improving communication, reducing staff workload, and finding ways to do more with less. In short, we asked: how can AI help us solve today's problems?

What is immediately clear is that the current digital and IT landscape across education is fragmented. Some institutions are AI-curious but lack the infrastructure or capacity to get started. Others are further along, experimenting with tools but without a coherent strategy. Many are still heavily reliant on legacy systems that don't integrate, lack automation, and absorb valuable staff time. Strategy documents may talk about "digital transformation," but few include a clear roadmap for implementing AI in a meaningful, sustainable way.

This book is a response to that inconsistency. It captures our approach, its successes and failures. It also offers suggested improvements to our action and implementation. It offers a practical, honest look at what it takes to introduce AI into an education setting, not as a silver bullet, but as a set of tools that, when deployed wisely, can transform how institutions operate. Drawing on lived experience, case studies, and emerging best practice, this book is designed to empower education leaders to make informed, strategic decisions about AI.

Operational efficiency isn't about doing everything faster. It's about doing the right things better and freeing up time, energy, and resources for what really matters: supporting students, staff, and communities. AI can help us get there. This book will show you how.

CHAPTER 1: WHY AI, WHY NOW?

In a time of tightening budgets, increasing workloads, and ever-rising expectations from students, parents, and regulatory bodies, the need for innovation in the education sector has never been more pressing. Institutions are being asked to do more with less, deliver exceptional learning experiences, uphold rigorous standards of safeguarding and accountability, maintain inclusive practices, and improve outcomes across increasingly diverse cohorts; all while navigating recruitment challenges and operational inefficiencies.

Publicly funded education is under strain. Funding increases have often failed to keep pace with inflation, particularly in the further education sector which although grant funded like schools (based on student numbers), lacks the same funding protection as them, where colleges are expected to act with the dynamism of businesses while being funded like public services. Staff workloads continue to grow, with administrative demands and compliance responsibilities eating into time that could be better spent on teaching, mentoring, or strategic improvement. Meanwhile, the competitive landscape has intensified, with more parents and students evaluating institutions not only on academic results but also on digital maturity, student experience, and graduate readiness.

At the same time, Artificial Intelligence (AI) has undergone a rapid evolution. Once confined to research labs and science fiction, AI is now a part of daily life, powering the tools we use to search, communicate, shop, and work. Breakthroughs in large language models (LLMs), image generation, machine learning, and natural language processing have propelled AI into mainstream business operations and the wider media. What was once complex and costly is now increasingly accessible, with user-friendly interfaces and Application Programming Interfaces (API's are a set of rules that allow different software applications to communicate and exchange data with each other), allowing for bespoke applications even in non-technical organisations. Suddenly, we are all expert authors who feel empowered to be able to write a book... right?!

The education sector is at a unique crossroads, an inflection point. While AI has been touted as a revolutionary force in teaching and learning, its less visible, but arguably more immediate, potential lies in transforming the operational backbone of our institutions. Automating repetitive tasks, streamlining data handling, reducing human error, and creating systems that can operate around the clock without fatigue, these are all outcomes AI can help deliver right now.

For my organisation, this wasn't just about keeping up with trends or experimenting with new gadgets. This was a strategic response to real-world pressures: staffing challenges, workload fatigue, inefficiencies in back-office systems, and the urgent desire to improve stakeholder experience across the board. Aligned to Kotter's model, we recognised the burning platform: persistent inefficiencies, staffing shortages, and a need to do more with less. Our vision was not to replace people with machines, but to empower our teams! To reduce the noise and admin load and allow our staff to focus on what they do best: delivering high-quality education, mentoring students, and shaping futures.

Harnessing the power of AI was not the destination, but it was the key to unlocking smarter, leaner, and more adaptive ways of working. As we looked at our strategic goals and the trajectory of the sector, the question was no longer "Why AI?" but "Why not now?"

"The time to really explore technology is when it's on its way toward getting good, if you invest and test it properly when most

still believe that it's a toy or a distraction, you put yourself in position to really reap its benefits when it's ready for Prime Time."

Salman Khan
Founder of "Khan Academy"
Author of *Brave New Words*

Seeing the Opportunity: Visionary Leadership and Strategic Insight

The decision to explore Artificial Intelligence (AI) at our College was not the result of a passing trend or an impulsive leap into the unknown. It was the product of careful, deliberate, and forward-thinking leadership, anchored by the Principal's strategic vision and a shared recognition among the Senior Leadership Team (SLT) that the time had come to be proactive and get ahead of the technology that would inevitably have an impact on the sector. Our AI journey began with a strategic dialogue that exemplified the Burke-Litwin Model in action.

By early 2024, it had become clear that many of our most persistent operational challenges stemmed from repetitive, time-consuming tasks that drained resources and were prone to human error. From enrolment administration to routine communications, the workload was rising while capacity remained flat. At the same time, we were facing increasing difficulties in recruiting and retaining staff in key support roles, particularly those at the lower end of our pay structure. The private sector, with its ability to offer more competitive salaries and flexible conditions, was drawing talent away from education, and the strain on existing teams was becoming untenable.

In this context, the Principal initiated what would become one of the most insightful and robust strategic conversations within a SLT that I had seen. Far from an echo chamber, the discussion was dynamic, challenging, and energising. Each voice in the room brought a different lens: curriculum, operations, IT, student services, staff and students' perspectives; and every viewpoint was tested, questioned, and refined. This aligns with McKinsey's 7S Framework, particularly the alignment of strategy, systems, and staff. We weren't merely bolting on new tech, we were assessing how AI could reinforce our culture, improve systems, and support our strategic goals. The debate was not about whether AI was "on trend," but about whether it was the right strategic move for the college at this moment in time.

It was, without question, one of the most intellectually rich and professionally rigorous conversations I've had the privilege to witness, let alone contribute to, in an educational setting. There was no groupthink, only critical engagement, a healthy dose of scepticism, and a shared ambition to future-proof our institution.

What emerged from that meeting was not a directive, but a conviction: that AI, if approached responsibly and strategically, could play a pivotal role in addressing our operational pressures. More than that, it could enable us to reimagine how we serve our students and staff. But can you imagine my fear, only having been in post for four months and I get told that I am going to lead our exploration of Artificial Intelligence, I knew nothing about AI…

AI presented itself not as a solution, but as a smart toolset, capable of streamlining burdensome tasks, reducing error, and creating the headroom our people needed to focus on meaningful work. The potential extended beyond efficiency: we saw an opportunity to make access to services smoother, information easier to find, and student interactions more personalised and timelier.

Guided by the Principal's vision, and shaped through this high-quality internal discourse, we began to explore how AI could be applied not only to operational functions, but to improve the overall experience of college life, for learners and staff alike. The discussion set the tone for everything that followed: open, ambitious, thoughtful, and grounded in our values. Values that prioritise a high-quality, holistic education for all.

This early conversation didn't just spark our AI journey; it defined the ethos by which we would undertake it: not chasing innovation for its own sake but harnessing it to serve a greater purpose.

Building from a Solid Foundation

We were in a fortunate position when we began exploring the role of AI in education. A critical insight from the Technology Acceptance Model (TAM) is that perceived usefulness and ease of use are central to adoption. Fortunately, we had already invested heavily in digital infrastructure, and much of it was robust, secure, and technically sound. Our staff and students were generally confident in their digital skills, and we had access to a wide range of platforms, from cloud-based learning environments to collaborative tools and our bespoke front-end to a management information system (MIS).

However, while our infrastructure was strong, it lacked cohesion. We were rich in tools but poor in integration, a classic case of misalignment in the "shared systems" aspect of the 7S Framework. We recognised that our digital infrastructure needed to evolve from a collection of standalone tools into an enabler of our strategic vision. What we didn't yet have was a clearly defined digital strategy, one that not only made sense of our digital environment but actively contributed to the delivery of our college's overarching strategic plan. Our digital tools were not being harnessed with shared purpose or direction. Instead, they existed in parallel with our strategic aims, rather than as a mechanism to help achieve them.

Like many educational institutions, we had accumulated a "typical" catalogue of legacy systems over time, some open-source and Linux-based, others proprietary or subscription-based. There were software licences being paid for that were rarely used, systems in place that only a handful of staff could operate, and processes that required staff to jump between multiple platforms to complete relatively simple tasks. In short, we had digital capability, but it wasn't working as hard or as smartly as it could have been.

This realisation was a pivotal moment. As a college committed to excellence, innovation, and student-centred outcomes, we knew our digital strategy couldn't be an afterthought. It had to be integrated with the delivery of our strategic plan. If our vision was to improve operational efficiency, increase access and equity, and deliver outstanding experiences for all stakeholders, then our digital tools had to be aligned with those same ambitions. Technology needed to support, not complicate, our processes. Our systems had to be more than functional; they had to be purposeful.

As part of our commitment to delivering a purposeful and resilient digital strategy, we also recognised the critical importance of strengthening our cybersecurity posture. With the integration of AI and increased reliance on cloud-based systems, safeguarding sensitive data, particularly that of our students and staff, became non-negotiable. At a time when digital crime was not only rising rapidly, but also targeting public sector organisations, achieving Cyber Essentials certification was highlighted as a key milestone in our strategy. It provides both a practical framework and an external benchmark to ensure that our systems, processes, and behaviours meet a recognised standard of protection. Importantly, we embedded cybersecurity into our digital strategy from the outset, not as an afterthought, but as a foundational layer. This alignment ensured that as we explored new technologies, we did so with confidence, accountability, and a clear understanding of the risks and responsibilities involved.

The potential introduction of AI became the catalyst we needed. It prompted us to look critically at what we already had, what was working, and where we were duplicating effort or missing opportunities. More importantly, it gave us the chance to start aligning our digital systems with our strategic goals, rationalising tools, streamlining platforms, and ensuring that each technological decision we made was intentional and impact driven.

We didn't throw everything out and start again. Instead, we treated our existing infrastructure as a foundation, a solid one, but ready for intelligent transformation. AI wasn't just about new capabilities; it was about coherence. It encouraged us to build a digital environment that not only functioned efficiently but actively supported the ambitions set out in our strategic plan.

The result was a new way of thinking: a shift from seeing digital as infrastructure, to seeing it as a strategy. And with that shift, we created the conditions for meaningful, measurable change.

From Curiosity to Commitment

As mentioned previously, our journey began not with a declaration, but with a series of open, high-level strategic conversations within the SLT. Conversations that mirror the 'knowledge–persuasion–decision' stages in Rogers' Diffusion of Innovation Theory. These discussions were grounded in curiosity, tempered by realism, and focused on the long-term sustainability of the college. We weren't simply interested in AI as a novelty; we were committed to exploring its feasibility, its risks, and critically… its potential rewards.

We looked broadly at the potential areas of application: business operations, cybersecurity, student support, and teaching and learning. But it quickly became clear that the most logical and impactful starting point would be our business services, such as finance, MIS, exams, estates, administration, and support functions. This decision was not made in isolation, nor was it about bypassing the classroom. It was strategic, practical, and aligned with the pressing needs of the college.

These departments were responsible for the kind of high-volume, low-variation tasks where generative AI and automation are particularly effective. Think data checking, data input, invoice processing, policy management, internal communications, report generation, and compliance-related workflows. Tasks that require consistency, accuracy, and speed, but not the nuance of pedagogical judgement or emotional intelligence. These were also the areas most affected by staff shortages and retention pressures, where gaps in resources had a tangible operational cost.

We knew from the outset that AI wasn't a magic wand, but it did offer clear, known strengths. At the time, generative AI models, particularly LLMs like ChatGPT, had demonstrated their power in handling structured data, summarising documents, generating templated text, translating between formats or languages, and responding to natural language queries. These capabilities aligned perfectly with many of the day-to-day demands of back-office operations. The opportunity wasn't to replace labour, but to remove friction: to reduce errors, standardise responses, and speed up tasks that previously drained valuable staff time.

It's important to note that, while the application of AI in teaching and learning was part of our longer-term vision, it was not our immediate priority. The national discourse at the time was preoccupied with the idea of AI replacing teachers, particularly the notion that it could automate marking and feedback, and provide personalised learning to all children. While I would argue that "teacher workload" is the single biggest threat to the current model of education, we knew it was too early for us to develop an AI solution to that issue at the time. Frankly, I hoped this was an issue that central government might address at scale, through regulation, funding, or national platforms, rather than a problem we would need to solve at an organisation level.

Our intent was different. We were focused on improving the college's operational core. If we could use AI to streamline administrative bottlenecks, mitigate some of the risk of staff turnover, and create headroom within overstretched teams, we could build a stronger, more resilient institution. And if we succeeded, we would also build confidence, both internally and externally, that AI could be a tool for meaningful, responsible change in education. This prioritisation echoes the TAM's focus on immediate, demonstrable benefit as a driver of trust and uptake.

This phased, purpose-led approach, from curiosity to commitment, became a hallmark of our strategy. It allowed us to test and learn, to invest wisely, and to ensure that our AI journey was not just exciting, but sustainable.

Seeking the Right Expertise

With a clear vision in place and strategic buy-in from the SLT, the next step in our journey was to bring in external expertise. We knew we were venturing into a rapidly evolving, highly technical space, and we needed partners who could do more than simply talk the talk. We needed true experts, people who could guide, challenge, and co-develop meaningful solutions tailored to the unique demands of a further education college.

So, we began exploring the market for AI and data science consultants, those with the credibility and capacity to help us explore and realise our ambitions. We reached out to thirteen different firms, casting the net wide to assess the breadth and quality of the marketplace. What we found was… mixed.

There were certainly some standout firms, credible, competent, and aligned with our values, but worryingly, there was also a considerable amount of noise. It quickly became clear that the market was awash with self-proclaimed "experts": chancers hoping to cash in on the AI gold rush, often with very little substance behind the pitch. Some proposals were impressive on the surface but flimsy when scrutinised. Others were strong technically but clearly lacked an understanding of the nuances and constraints of the education sector. The variation in quality, experience, and crucially, price was astonishing.

And the costs? At the time the costs made me gulp.

Coming from a background in a local secondary school, where every expenditure had to be justified line by line and non-routine capital expenditure was a thing of myths, the figures being discussed felt eye-watering. I remember looking at the estimates for the deep-dive analyses and agent development and feeling a wave of panic. Could we really spend this much? What if it didn't work? What if we got it wrong?

On the surface, the cost of a deep dive into our operational challenges and the development of bespoke AI agents was expensive; however, upon reflection, they were significantly lower than the expense of licensing a commercial software as a service (SaaS) product for a number of years. Many of these off-the-shelf solutions offer attractive interfaces and promises of integration, yet in practice, they only address around 60 per cent of the actual problem. The remaining 40 per cent still demands manual workarounds, additional systems, or process compromises. By contrast, our tailored agents would not only meet our specific needs with pinpoint accuracy but could also evolve alongside our workflows, ensuring long-term value without the perpetual cost of third-party software subscriptions, creating barriers to exit. This reinforced our belief that meaningful transformation isn't just about adopting new tools, it's about owning the solution.

But my Principal wasn't fazed.

He understood the high costs of good consultants; he also knew that they weren't anything like the consultancy costs seen in the commercial sector. He understood that they were not a risk, but an investment. A credible consultant, who you trust and who brings specialist expertise, can unlock value far beyond their fee, transforming complex problems into actionable solutions with lasting impact.

This confidence in our pursuit was also underpinned by the lean and efficient nature of our workforce. Operating at a rate of 60 per cent of grant allocation to staff expenditure, we run a tight ship and this allowed us to invest in supporting those staff through the procurement of specialist support. The Principal reminded me that innovation carries a price tag, and that if we wanted to be bold, we had to be prepared to commit.

More importantly, he offered something rare in leadership: permission to try, and room to fail...

He said, clearly and without hesitation, that some of what we develop will almost certainly be superseded by the pace of the technology. Some tools might become redundant. Some ideas might not work as planned. That wouldn't be seen as a failure, more a lesson learned, that was the nature of working with new and emerging technology. His message was clear: our responsibility was to explore the possibilities, make well informed and balanced decisions, and learn as we go.

That reassurance gave me a freedom I hadn't experienced before. It gave me the confidence to run with the vision, to leap into the unknown, and to build something genuinely innovative, without crippling fear of being second-guessed or penalised for imperfect outcomes.

This is where Kotter's steps 4 and 5, communicating the vision and empowering broad-based action, came into play. Our Principal gave the project the political capital it needed. He also offered something rare in leadership: psychological safety. There was explicit permission to explore, test, and, even occasionally, fail.

In the end, we appointed two external consultants who stood out for their knowledge, credibility, experience, complementary strengths, and shared ethos. The first focused on developing bespoke AI agents, with deep technical expertise in LLMs, API integration (this is explained in chapter 3), and secure deployment within our digital environment. The second explored the potential of migrating systems to the cloud and using the tools offered by our enterprise software partner to improve efficiency and collaboration.

These consultants didn't just provide technical support, they offered an external lens that helped us challenge our assumptions, view our own systems with fresh perspective and create a meaningful digital strategy. Their involvement helped us to assess the current state of operations, spot duplication and inefficiencies, and pinpoint where AI could deliver a meaningful return on investment, in terms of stakeholder experience.

But more than that, they helped catalyse a mindset shift within me: from caution to curiosity, from possibility to action. And it was the unwavering belief of our Principal and the rest of the SLT, their willingness to back me with both trust and resource, that made all of it possible.

Intent Over Impulse: Leading with Purpose, Not Hype

Importantly, as mentioned previously, our engagement with AI wasn't driven by trend-chasing or the fear of being left behind. In a sector where new technologies frequently arrive with great fanfare, only to fade away once their novelty wears off, having made little to no impact beyond a significant dent in education spending, we were determined to take a different approach. We didn't want to pursue innovation for its own sake. We wanted to lead with purpose.

One of the most dangerous traps in digital transformation is adopting technology without clarity of purpose. We've all seen it, shiny tools that gather dust because they weren't tied to real needs. Remember the interactive whiteboard that soon adorned every classroom wall in the country? Only to become a glorified projector screen! Our strategy, as detailed throughout this book, was rooted in aligning every AI use case with an organisational challenge, consistent with Kotter's sixth step: generating short-term wins.

In a world where change fatigue is real and trust in "EdTech" is fragile, intentionality matters. Building on the leadership approach outlined already, we maintained a focus on pragmatic implementation, starting small and scaling what worked. We weren't chasing headlines. We were pursuing smart efficiency.

As previously mentioned, our vision for AI was clear from the outset: to make us more efficient, more responsive, and better prepared for the demands of the future. But just as importantly, we wanted to do so in a way that was aligned with our values, respectful of our staff, and mindful of our context. That meant resisting the temptation to jump at every shiny new tool or platform. It meant being strategic, measured, and intentional. If I am honest, I needed the grounding of the rest of the SLT at this point, excited by my new-found passion for an emerging technology, keen to make an impact in my new role, I wanted to run when I needed to walk.

Too often in education, institutions feel pressure to adopt the latest technology because it's what everyone else appears to be doing, or because vendors promise "revolutionary" outcomes, "transforming" the sector… But adopting AI without clarity of purpose risks turning innovation into a distraction. It consumes energy, erodes staff trust, and delivers little in the way of lasting value. We were determined not to fall into that trap.

Instead, we focused on delivering meaningful change, not reacting to a trend. We made a conscious decision to start small, test thoroughly, and scale only what worked. We created room to experiment without the pressure of perfection. We remained grounded in our mission and strategic plan, ensuring that any AI adoption was tied directly to real challenges we faced, and measurable outcomes we wanted to achieve.

Conclusion: Purpose, Not Panic

This chapter of our journey is, at its heart, about intent. It was never about hype. It was about purposeful transformation, driven by clear-eyed leadership and grounded in practical insight. The Burke-Litwin model reminds us that true change happens when strategy, structure, systems, and leadership are aligned, and that's exactly what we built.

We began with questions, not answers. But what followed was a structured, theory-informed, and values-driven approach that prepared us for the next chapter: moving from foundation to function.

We wanted to lead, not follow. We wanted to explore the possibilities of AI to meet our issues, not to deploy it for the sake of headlines or marketing materials, but to genuinely understand where it could make a meaningful difference. And above all, we wanted to ensure that any technology we adopted served our people, our staff, our students, and our community, not the other way around.

AI is powerful, but it is also neutral. Its value comes from how it is used, why it is used, and who it is designed to benefit. Our approach was grounded in the belief that education should shape technology to fit its values, not bend its values to fit the technology.

In the chapters that follow, I detail how we translated this strategic intent into practical action. I share how we began with business services and operational pain points, how we developed our first AI agents, and how this thoughtful, deliberate approach is now shaping a whole-college journey toward what I call smart efficiency... a future where innovation is purposeful, inclusive, and sustainable.

Chapter 1: 😊 What We Learned

- AI can address immediate operational pain points in education, not just long-term pedagogical ambitions.
- A strategic, values-led approach beats trend-chasing every time.
- Early leadership conversations should be intellectually rich, inclusive, and aligned to institutional challenges.
- Frameworks like Kotter and Burke-Litwin can provide structure to innovation and help avoid tech for tech's sake.

Chapter 1: 💡 Key Reflection Questions

- What operational or cultural challenges within your institution signal a genuine need for innovation?
- Are your leadership discussions about AI inclusive, strategic, and intellectually rigorous?
- How well does your current digital infrastructure align with your organisation's mission and strategic goals?
- Where in your organisation is there curiosity about AI, and what's preventing progress?
- Is your institution approaching AI as a trend to follow or as a purposeful transformation?
- Are you using any structured change models (e.g., Burke-Litwin, Kotter, ADKAR) to support implementation?
- Have you created psychological safety for your team to explore, experiment, and learn with AI?
- Where can AI free up time and reduce admin so your staff can focus on high-value work?

CHAPTER 2: LAYING THE GROUNDWORK

Every transformation should begin with a strong foundation. For us, our groundwork for AI implementation wasn't rooted in technical ambition alone, it was anchored in clarity of purpose, data-driven insight, and a deep commitment to responsible innovation. This aligns with the "Unfreeze" stage of Lewin's Change Model, where existing mindsets and systems are critically examined in preparation for meaningful change.

Before a single line of code was written or an AI agent deployed, we took a step back to ask fundamental questions: What problems are we trying to solve? Where could AI make the greatest impact? And how can we ensure that its benefits are delivered equitably, securely, and sustainably?

We understood early on that AI, for all its potential, is not a universally accepted solution. There were, understandably, sceptics among staff, some concerned about job security, others cautious about data privacy, ethics, or the pace of technological change. These reactions reflected the "Awareness" and "Desire" stages of the ADKAR Model, highlighting the importance of engaging hearts and minds before introducing tools. In the wider education sector, there was no shortage of scaremongering: warnings about students cheating, jobs being automated away, or AI replacing the judgement and care of educators. These concerns couldn't be ignored, and most importantly, we didn't try to.

Taking people with us was paramount. Our approach was aligned with Kotter's principle of building a guiding coalition and communicating the vision. We recognised that sustained change required trust, transparency, and collaboration across multiple stakeholder levels.

We knew that successful implementation would depend not just on technical capability, but on trust, transparency, and collective ownership. That meant listening as much as leading. It meant creating space for honest dialogue, addressing fears without defensiveness, and ensuring that AI was framed not as a threat, but as a tool, one that could ease workloads, improve processes, and enhance the human aspects of college life, rather than replace them.

This people-first approach shaped everything we did. We didn't chase quick wins or rush flashy pilots. Instead, we invested time in understanding our organisation's needs, pain points, and priorities. We conducted operational deep dives, interviewing key staff about their pinch points, we reviewed data on staff workload and system performance, and carefully mapped areas where AI could make a tangible difference. Alongside this, we strengthened our governance structures, began working towards Cyber Essentials certification, and embedded cybersecurity and ethical design principles into our digital strategy.

In doing so, we created not just a technical foundation, but a cultural one, a shared understanding that AI would be developed with care, deployed with purpose, and continuously evaluated through the lens of our mission, values, and people.

Mapping the Landscape

The first tangible step in our AI journey was a comprehensive audit of our business services, an honest, detailed look at how our college was operating behind the scenes, carried out by an external consultant. This mirrors the diagnostic approach within the Burke-Litwin Model, which emphasises the importance of assessing organisational systems and workflows before undertaking transformational change.

The consultant began by asking fundamental questions: Where are we spending the most time? Which processes are most prone to error? Where are the staff feeling the greatest strain? And crucially, where are we least efficient, not because of a lack of effort, but because of outdated systems, repetitive manual work, or labour-intensive processes?

This exercise wasn't about criticism. Far from it. It was about empowering our teams. It was about recognising that our support staff were often doing exceptional work under considerable pressure, trying to deliver high standards with tools and systems that hadn't kept pace with the demands placed upon them. This process also aligned with digital maturity assessment models, such as the "Jisc framework", which encourages institutions to assess their digital capabilities, skills, and infrastructure before implementing large-scale change. We knew that if we wanted to bring about meaningful change, we had to start by listening to the experts already in the building.

The AI consultant we brought on board led a series of structured, in-depth conversations with the managers of each support service area: catering, MIS, exams, marketing, finance, HR, estates, IT, administration, and more. These were not surface-level interviews; they were working sessions where managers were invited to walk through their workflows, highlight their pain points, and talk candidly about what was and wasn't working for them and their teams.

What stood out most was the openness and honesty in the room. The consultant asked insightful, probing questions, but it was our managers who led the conversation. They were experts in their services. They knew the sticking points, the unnecessary duplication, the moments where systems failed or effort exceeded output. Their willingness to share challenges so transparently made these sessions incredibly valuable. Not just for the consultant, but for me, new in post and keen to understand the teams and their work.

For my part, I deliberately took a step back. I attended every session, not as a leader instructing change, but as a learner. I sat quietly, listening carefully, observing the dynamics of each team and trying to deepen my own understanding, not just of where AI might fit, but of how our college really operated at ground level. This was as much about growing my insight as it was about scoping future innovation.

What emerged from those sessions was a clear picture of where we were struggling, not because of poor performance, but because of the limits of human capacity in a system that had grown increasingly complex. Tasks like document verification, data checking, and data entry, all essential, all resource-intensive, and many of them crying out for intelligent automation.

Importantly, these audits gave us focus. It allowed us to identify the pinch points that mattered most to the people doing the work. And in doing so, it shaped the foundation for everything that followed: the creation of our first AI agents, the development of targeted solutions, and the rollout of tools that were built not just for efficiency, but for impact.

This wasn't a top-down transformation, it was a collaborative, respectful process grounded in lived experience. And it was in these early conversations that the real potential of AI began to take shape, not as a distant, abstract concept, but as a practical, achievable pathway to relieving pressure, improving systems, and making people's working lives better.

It was all about the staff experience...

Bringing in External Experts

As previously stated, to ensure objectivity and access the latest thinking in AI applications, we made the strategic decision to partner with two external organisations. This partnership reflected the "Knowledge" and "Persuasion" stages of Rogers' Diffusion of Innovation Theory, where early adopters seek external insight and validation before committing to change. This wasn't just about outsourcing expertise, it was about enriching our internal capacity with fresh perspectives, technical depth, and a critical eye.

The first was an AI consultancy specialising in the development of bespoke solutions. They brought an advanced understanding of LLMs, automation, and system integration.

The second was an enterprise software-focused technology partner, selected for their deep knowledge of cloud infrastructure, workspace optimisation, and emerging tools like commercial LLMs. Their role was to assess the potential of migrating our systems to the cloud, help us create a meaningful digital strategy, while also exploring how we could unlock more value from our existing licenses and infrastructure. They also had the core role of delivering consistent staff training on utilising tools offered by our enterprise software partner and the integration into our regularly used applications.

Crucially, both consultants brought something we didn't have internally: the ability to be both expert and objective. They weren't bound by legacy workflows, inherited systems or internal assumptions. They asked questions we hadn't thought to ask, challenged processes we'd long accepted as normal, and benchmarked our current state against what was possible, not just what was familiar. Their embedded, co-design approach reflected best practice in agile transformation, where user-centred design, iteration, and cross-functional feedback loops are prioritised.

They didn't limit their approach to interviews or surface-level reviews. Instead, they embedded themselves in our college environment. They shadowed teams in real time, observed how tasks were carried out, and reviewed historical records and performance data. They worked side by side with our managers, exploring pinch points, inefficiencies, and opportunities, always with respect for the teams, and always with a focus on practical improvement.

What set them apart was their dual lens. On one hand, they could identify where existing tools might already offer a solution, perhaps underused features in our MIS, or automations available within our enterprise software that hadn't yet been adopted. On the other hand, they brought the capability to design bespoke AI solutions where none existed, tailored agents that could plug gaps, integrate across systems, and adapt to the unique demands of further education. From my time in secondary education, I had become frustrated with commercial tools that do 60 per cent to 80 per cent of a job or function, longing for development to "just do the job properly", something that never happened. Instead, we in education tend to procure system after system or solution after solution, aimed at getting closer to improved efficiency. Ultimately, nothing ever gives the full solution, nothing ever meets the need… "This time it could be different", that was my thought process.

The output of the work carried out by the AI consultancy company was a detailed operational map. They presented a comprehensive analysis that identified 107 discrete functions where AI (or simply automation) could drive improvement, whether through increased efficiency, enhanced accuracy, better user experience, or a combination of all three. This move from qualitative insight to quantifiable targets reflected the ADKAR "Knowledge" and "Ability" phases, translating awareness into skills and capabilities.

These findings weren't presented as a scattergun list of ideas; they were organised, rationalised, and prioritised. The 107 opportunities were carefully clustered into 26 unique solutions, called "agents". We explore what we mean by agents later, but each one had a clear rationale, expected benefit, and potential ROI.

This clarity was powerful. It gave us a tangible development roadmap, allowing us to make informed decisions about where to invest first, which problems to solve early, and where to expect the quickest returns. But more than that, it gave us confidence, because these insights weren't theoretical, and they weren't generated in isolation. They were the result of collaborative, data-driven analysis involving the very people who would go on to use these tools in their daily work.

By drawing on external expertise in such a targeted and strategic way, we avoided the trap of building solutions in search of a problem. Instead, we let our operational reality drive the innovation. And that, ultimately, is what made the outcomes so impactful.

Early Strategic Choices

With the data in hand, 107 suitable functions, grouped into 26 unique "agent" use cases, we reached a critical juncture. We had clarity, direction, and more ideas than we could possibly implement at once. Here, we applied principles from Kotter's Step 6, generate short-term wins, by identifying which agents were likely to deliver visible, early success. Now came the harder question: Where do we begin?

We took the findings back to a SLT meeting. What followed was a robust discussion about ethics, business needs, value for money and expectations. It was clear we couldn't proceed with all 26 use cases simultaneously. Each one would require development time, staff engagement, training, testing, and a support plan. The challenge was to balance ambition with focus, to choose the solutions that would deliver the biggest impact and serve as early proof points for the wider college. Perhaps the greatest challenge of that conversation was, what would we develop that wouldn't be superseded by the rapid development of the tech?

In that SLT meeting, we asked ourselves some key questions:

- Which agents would deliver measurable, visible gains?
- Where were staff feeling the most pressure now?
- Which processes were causing repeated frustration or delays?
- Which tools could be built quickly, trialled safely, and scaled easily?

The answer was easily reached, supporting the business services that would have the most positive impact. These departments were the backbone of college operations, and they were under constant strain. Their tasks were high-volume, rules-based, and prone to human error. These were the very conditions where generative AI thrived. This decision aligned with the "early adopter" phase of innovation diffusion theory, where new tools are introduced into environments that are structurally and culturally ready. Success here would deliver tangible benefits and, just as importantly, build internal confidence in the potential of AI.

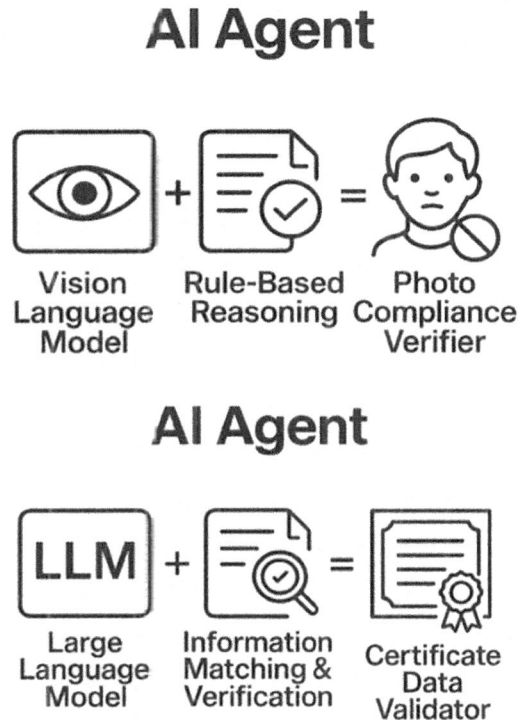

Figure 1: Illustration of capabilities combined to create agents.

We also discussed which agents we were most sceptical about. Some ideas were exciting on paper but raised concerns in practice, either because they involved too much technical complexity (when we hadn't begun unlocking the capabilities yet), touched on sensitive data, or risked creating false expectations. There were animated conversations around agents like absence prediction, behavioural insights, and student well-being monitoring, ideas that had promise, but where the risk of misunderstanding, overreach, or ethical missteps was higher. We agreed to park those for a later phase, when our understanding and governance structures were more developed.

Other use cases generated strong consensus. Tools like the GCSE Results Agent, Certificate AI, and the Student Buddy (our digital student knowledge base) were seen as high-value, low-risk. They addressed real pain points and were straightforward to scope. These became our early focus, not because they were the most innovative, but because they were the most *necessary*. Whilst being easier to develop the capabilities. Capabilities that once unlocked, would themselves offer new opportunities. The illustration (figure 1) is a visual illustration of agent development and unlocking capabilities. It shows that when you combine two or more capabilities to create a bespoke output, you have created an "agent".

From these conversations, we made several foundational decisions that would shape the rest of our journey:

Start With Business Services:

These teams dealt with the kinds of repetitive, structured tasks that were ideally suited to early-stage AI solutions, particularly those powered by the APIs and large language models available at the time. Our aim wasn't just to implement AI, it was to implement it well, and that meant aligning our ambitions with what the technology could realistically deliver in its current state.

Business services functions involved high volumes of standardised data, time-consuming documentation, rigid processes, and a constant need for accuracy and consistency. These were the perfect conditions for automation, not because the work was unimportant, but because it was predictable, structured, and often overburdened with manual input.

But we were also pragmatic. We understood the limitations of the application programming interfaces (APIs – we explain what these are later on), and AI models that we had access to. These tools were powerful, but they were not all-knowing or universally adaptable. They worked best when applied to narrow tasks, with well-defined inputs and clearly structured outputs. So, we made a deliberate decision to prioritise agent development in areas where current AI capabilities were most likely to succeed, text processing, data handling, templated communication, search-and-retrieve tasks, and rule-based decision trees.

By focusing on operational functions where AI could drive efficiency gains within the guardrails of what the APIs could already do, we increased the likelihood of success and reduced the risk of misaligned expectations. This wasn't just a technical decision; it was a strategic one. Early success would validate the investment, build confidence among staff, and lay the groundwork for tackling more complex, nuanced use cases later, such as those involving teaching and learning, behavioural insights, or personalised student support.

This approach allowed us to build momentum without overreaching. It enabled us to demonstrate immediate, measurable improvements, reduced labour hours, fewer errors, and quicker turnaround times. All while deepening our internal understanding of AI integration. In doing so, we created the space, structure, and capability to scale with confidence when the next generation of tools emerged.

Focus on Customisation and Control:

From the outset, we made a conscious decision to develop all AI agents within our own digital tenancy. This wasn't just a technical preference, it was a strategic choice, rooted in our values, our data privacy expectations, our responsibilities, and our long-term vision for sustainable digital transformation.

By retaining control over the environment, rather than outsourcing core functionality to third-party hosted platforms, we positioned ourselves to take ownership not only of the tools themselves, but of the rules that govern their use. We weren't simply deploying AI; we were shaping it to fit our needs, our context, and our community. By owning the development of bespoke solutions, we eliminated the need for costly annual licences and reduced our dependence on external vendors developing universal solutions for the masses. We remained agnostic, removing barriers to exit and ensuring that our tools could evolve on our terms, not someone else's roadmap.

One of the most common misconceptions about AI is that it's either "on" or "off", a binary tool that either runs or doesn't. In reality, leveraging AI responsibly is about designing the boundaries: defining what it can do, what it shouldn't do, and under what conditions it operates. Building our own agents gave us the power to implement enhanced controls and safeguards that are tailored to the educational setting, our staff, and our learners.

Many of our agents were specifically designed to avoid hallucinations or unsafe outputs. Each one operates with a defined confidence threshold, if the model returns a confidence score below that threshold, the response defaults to:

"I am not able to answer that question."

This is achieved via a mix of prompt engineering, logic-layer filtering, and rules-based restrictions. This "100 per cent accuracy" policy was embedded in the logic of many of our agents. If an agent wasn't certain of the correctness of its response, it wouldn't guess or hallucinate. This design choice not only upheld the integrity of the information provided but also built trust among users, who quickly came to understand that these tools were governed by rigour, not speculation.

Importantly all responses from our agents are logged for audit and monitoring purposes, ensuring traceability and safeguarding integrity.

We also implemented restrictions on output types, such as disabling the generation of images or video, and applied strict rules around what data the agents could access, process, or store. Because the agents operated entirely within our digital environment, all activity was GDPR compliant by design. Sensitive student or staff data never left our ecosystem, and we had full visibility over how the tools were being used.

This approach also had clear financial and operational benefits. By avoiding reliance on third-party tools with opaque data usage policies and costly licence structures, we could reduce long-term costs while enhancing transparency and control. Our digital estate remained coherent, auditable, and aligned with our broader cyber security and data governance commitments.

Ultimately, this commitment to customisation and control allowed us to turn AI from a general-purpose capability into a strategic asset, one that aligned with our values, met our compliance obligations, and was designed from the ground up to serve our people, not the other way around.

Develop Our Own LLM Front End:

Rather than always having to direct staff (and in the future, students) to public-facing tools like ChatGPT, Gemini or Copilot, we made the strategic decision to build our own interface to a LLM – "Bespoke LLM", tailored specifically to our environment, our values, and our community. This wasn't just a branding exercise; it was a foundational decision rooted in trust, security, and long-term sustainability. More details on this agent are provided in chapter 3. For now, let's consider the financial benefits of this solution.

Commercial LLM tools often require costly per-user monthly licences, creating a significant barrier to scale, especially for educational institutions with large student cohorts and limited budgets. By building Bespoke LLM in-house and operating it via API calls on a usage-based model, we adopted a far more financially viable "pay-as-you-go" approach. Instead of fixed monthly costs, we paid only for what was used, dramatically reducing overheads while allowing us to grow the tool sustainably and incrementally.

In short, Bespoke LLM wasn't just an interface... it was a reflection of our digital values: secure, ethical, inclusive, scalable, and grounded in the real-world demands of education. It demonstrated that AI could be not only powerful, but also safe, purposeful, and affordable, when it is owned, shaped, and governed by the institution it serves.

Red Team Every Agent:

From the outset, we agreed that rigorous testing was non-negotiable. In education, especially when dealing with AI (at a time of little to no guidance), we cannot afford to release tools that haven't been robustly challenged. The stakes are too high. Accuracy, reliability, safeguarding, and public trust are paramount. That's why we implemented a formal red team process for every AI agent we developed.

Before any tool was rolled out into a live environment, it was first deployed in a sandbox environment (an isolated testing space where it could be safely examined without risk to operational systems or real data). But we didn't just perform internal technical checks. We created dedicated red teams, composed of a diverse group of stakeholders, including staff from different departments, digital specialists, safeguarding leads, and carefully selected students. Their role was critical: to try and break the tool...

We specifically tasked red team members with pushing each AI agent to its limits, feeding it edge cases, malformed prompts, deliberately confusing queries, and, most importantly, inappropriate questions. These included safeguarding-sensitive scenarios, policy violations, and examples of topics no AI agent in a college setting should ever attempt to answer, such as requests for advice about drug use, self-harm, pornography, or violence. The question we asked ourselves throughout was clear: If someone tried to misuse this tool, would it fail safely?

This wasn't paranoia, it was prudence. We knew that if an agent ever responded inappropriately to a student's prompt, the safeguarding and reputational consequences could be catastrophic.

To mitigate this risk, we designed our red teaming to be ruthless by design, not to catch out our developers, but to make our tools better. These teams were encouraged to challenge the assumptions behind each agent's design, find vulnerabilities in its prompt logic, test its accuracy, and identify any unintended behaviours or potential for misuse.

In many ways, red teaming became as much a cultural safeguard as a technical one. It gave the staff and students a sense of shared ownership and accountability, and it helped build confidence that the tools were not only fit for purpose but were also tested through the lens of real-world usage and real student behaviour.

Crucially, the feedback from red teams directly influenced how agents were refined and improved before deployment. It helped us identify where to implement stronger prompt controls, where additional filtering was required, and where the agent needed clearer instructions to avoid hallucinations or ambiguous responses.

This process wasn't just a phase, it was a structured layer and a core part of our AI governance model. It sent a clear message across the college: we take safety, integrity, and user trust seriously, and we are willing to delay a release, rework a tool, or even scrap an idea entirely if it doesn't meet our standards. This stage aligned with the "Refreeze" in Lewin's model, embedding new tools into policy, culture, and systems while continuously evaluating outcomes.

This methodical, values-driven approach helped us avoid the two most common traps in AI deployment: rushing in too fast, and building tools that no one asked for. It kept our focus on solving real problems, one step at a time, while creating the cultural and technical infrastructure to scale safely and confidently in the future.

Building a Culture of AI Readiness

Technology alone wouldn't deliver meaningful change. We knew from the very beginning that the success of our AI journey would not be determined by how clever the tools were, but by how well we brought people with us. That meant being transparent, inclusive, and intentional in our approach, not just in what we built, but in how we communicated, trained, and supported those expected to use it.

A key part of this cultural groundwork came from the leadership team. SLT discussions around AI weren't just functional, they were strategic, challenging, and intellectually rich. Every proposed agent, policy, and approach was interrogated thoroughly. Risks were examined from all angles: safeguarding, workload, pedagogy, data governance, and reputational integrity. This rigour helped set the tone for the rest of the college: thoughtful, measured, and people-first.

Alongside this, we invested heavily in continuous professional development (CPD). If AI was going to become a part of everyday college life, our staff needed time and space to explore what that meant. We organised AI-focused INSET days, delivered practical workshops, and ran regular drop-in sessions where staff could ask questions, test new tools, and share their experiences. We brought in external speakers, showcased early wins from departments already using agents, and provided step-by-step guidance to ensure no one felt left behind. Importantly, our CPD offer was not one-size-fits-all, it ranged from high-level strategy discussions to hands-on support with prompt writing, depending on the needs of each team.

These activities reflected the Jisc Digital Capability Framework and the Technology Acceptance Model, investing in confidence and competence to build adoption.

But none of this would have worked without considered communication. We took great care in how we spoke about AI, not just in tone, but in language and substance. We made it clear from the outset what AI could do, but equally what it couldn't. We tackled misconceptions head-on, dispelled the myths fuelled by mainstream media, and regularly emphasised that these tools were not designed to replace staff, but to support them.

We held open forums and Q&A sessions with both staff and eventually with groups of students, creating safe spaces for questions, concerns, and feedback. We shared roadmaps, invited staff to test tools before launch, and celebrated the contributions of those who had helped shape our early agents. We communicated often, clearly, and honestly, acknowledging that this was new territory for many, and that uncertainty was natural.

This early focus on culture and communication paid dividends. Staff didn't seem to feel threatened by the changes, we brought them into the process. They weren't passive recipients of new systems; they were collaborators. They helped to test agents, critique outputs, identify flaws, and shape future iterations. Their insights didn't just build better tools, they built trust, engagement, and a shared sense of ownership over the college's digital direction.

By aligning strategic leadership, meaningful CPD, and open communication, we laid the cultural foundation that would support not only the first wave of AI adoption, but every stage of innovation that followed.

From Foundations to First Builds

By June 2024, the first of our AI agents was ready for demonstration. For me, it was a milestone that came with a mixture of pride, relief, and awe, because reaching that point had required an extraordinary amount of work, collaboration, and trust. I felt that I had achieved something I never imagined I would, in a field I knew little about – I felt (perhaps for the first time) that I could not only do my new role, but possibly do it well.

The pace at which we had moved was nothing short of remarkable. In just a few months, we had progressed from high-level strategic discussions to hands-on development, from deep-dive operational audits to fully functioning AI prototypes. Along the way, we had navigated complex decision-making, embedded robust governance, conducted extensive red-team testing, and shaped entirely new workflows from the ground up. For everyone involved, this had been an intense period of innovation, learning, and hard graft...

The sheer volume of work that went into those first few agents cannot be overstated. Each one represented hundreds of conversations, lines of code, red lines crossed out and rewritten, ideas tested and reworked, and hours spent refining the smallest of user interactions. And yet, the momentum never stalled. Staff gave their time generously, despite the pressures of their day jobs. Students contributed insightfully through testing and feedback. Our consultants became embedded partners. And the SLT remained steadfast, holding the vision and providing the space and support needed to move at pace without compromising on quality. Their critical challenge ensured that I, and indeed the developments, remained on track, safe and ethical. Upon reflection, that support was essential. When you are that close to the development, the exciting new technology and its flashy capabilities, it is easy to become distracted, to cut corners or to deviate from the scope of the agent.

The early tools, like the GCSE Results Agent, Student Buddy and Bespoke LLM, delivered immediate, measurable results. It is far too early to talk about meaningful quantitative data to demonstrate the return on our investment. However, we could with some agents, like the GCSE Results Agent which saved 93 labour hours during the enrolment period, while later Certificate AI reduced a previously arduous annual process by over 300 hours. But these were more than efficiency wins. They were proof of concept, not just to us but more astoundingly for the sector. They demonstrated that our model worked: identify a real problem, build a smart solution, test it thoroughly, and roll it out with the right support.

Importantly, these tools did more than solve problems, they started to shift mindsets. They gave our staff something tangible to see, use, and believe in. They weren't abstract slides in a strategy deck; they were working solutions, built for our college, delivering value from day one.

Our strategic evolution moved us from passive users of commercial tools to active creators of bespoke AI solutions. This transition brought control, flexibility, and deeper alignment with our operational goals.

Rather than relying on vendor roadmaps, we built the tools we needed, when and how we needed them. This cultural and technical shift redefined how we view digital transformation: not as something bought, but as something built.

Leading by Example: A Strategic Investment in Premium Education Licenses

As a SLT, we recognised early on the growing risk posed by staff inadvertently inputting sensitive or confidential data into free, unsecured large language models. Something that I still hear is happening regularly in education. Aware of the time it would take to develop our Bespoke LLM, we needed a quick solution. To address this, we made a bold and strategic decision: to purchase a premium education licence from our enterprise software partner, for every member of staff whilst we built our own solution. This proactive move ensured that all AI interactions across the organisation were fully compliant with GDPR and data protection regulations, while simultaneously empowering staff to work more efficiently and creatively with cutting-edge AI tools.

This commitment to secure responsible AI use positioned us as the largest procurer of such licences globally, a milestone that not only underlined our reputation as a pioneer in digital transformation within the education sector, but also gave us leverage to negotiate a better deal with the supplier.

We built our entire AI infrastructure within our cloud platform, enabling us to leverage its full suite of APIs and tools to maximise the benefits.

To ensure widespread adoption and confident use, as part of an agreement to purchase licences, we received regular, role-specific training for all staff from our partner. This included hands-on workshops in using the AI-powered tools on offer, including the newly released integration across their other applications and new features and tools as they were released. These sessions helped demystify AI and embedded a culture of experimentation and digital fluency across the college.

This bold approach did more than support internal operations, it captured the attention of our enterprise software provider. What followed was the opportunity to build a partnership with them unlike any other. This partnership marked not just a technological endorsement, but a shared commitment to shaping the future of education through responsible, innovative AI use.

Conclusion: Culture Before Code

The success of our early AI implementation did not rest on cutting-edge technology alone. It was built on careful groundwork, on honest evaluation, strategic prioritisation, and a deep respect for the people who make our college function. By aligning our efforts with established models of organisational change and innovation, Lewin's foundational stages of change, the Burke-Litwin framework for systemic alignment, Kotter's roadmap for transformation, and the ADKAR model for individual adoption, we ensured that our approach was not just innovative, but sustainable.

This chapter was about more than laying infrastructure. It was about laying trust. We took the time to understand where AI could genuinely add value, to build the case for change from the inside out, and to give our staff the tools, confidence, and clarity they needed to engage with this transformation meaningfully. By the time our first agents were deployed, the technology wasn't the surprising part; the cultural shift was. Staff didn't resist the tools; they helped build them. The students involved didn't fear the innovation; they tested and refined it. The groundwork we laid wasn't flashy, but it was fundamental. It created the conditions not just for success, but for scale.

The groundwork had been laid. The team was aligned. The culture was shifting. The technology was taking shape, not as a standalone innovation, but as part of a wider, human-centred transformation. This marked the transition from "Trial" to "Adoption" in the Diffusion of Innovation lifecycle.

What came next was the realisation of our vision: a smarter, leaner, more responsive college. A community where AI was no longer something distant or daunting, but something ours, built with purpose, governed with care, and always designed to work for people, not instead of them.

Chapter 2: 👥 What We Learned

- Meaningful change begins with honest evaluation, not new tools.
- Listening to staff and mapping lived pain points builds trust and reveals hidden inefficiencies.
- Bringing in the right external partners strengthens internal capacity and challenges assumptions.
- Culture-building, transparency, and cybersecurity readiness are non-negotiables for sustainable AI adoption.

Chapter 2: 💡 Key Reflection Questions

- Have you clearly identified the specific problems AI could help solve in your organisation?
- How are you involving staff in the early stages of AI exploration to build trust and gather insight?
- What methods are you using to map operational inefficiencies and workload bottlenecks?
- Do you have the right external partners to challenge assumptions and bring fresh expertise?
- How are ethical considerations, data protection, and cybersecurity being addressed from the outset?
- Are you prioritising tools that meet real needs over those that simply appear impressive?
- What structures do you have in place to govern, test, and red-team AI agents before deployment?
- How are you preparing your culture, not just your technology, for sustainable AI adoption?

CHAPTER 3: BUILDING AI FROM THE INSIDE OUT

With a strong foundation in place and a clear, data-informed roadmap of potential use cases, the next phase of our journey was about turning opportunity into reality. We had diagnosed the problems. We had secured buy-in, built trust, and laid the groundwork. Now it was time to develop the tools that would bring our vision of smart efficiency to life.

This stage marked a shift, from planning to production. It was no longer about exploring what AI might do for us, but about building tools that could start delivering impact here and now. The real test was not in strategy documents or sandbox ideas, but in whether we could create working agents that made a measurable difference to staff workload, student experience, and operational resilience.

What set our approach apart was our unwavering commitment to building AI tools to solve our problems. As explained in the previous chapters. We deliberately avoided purchasing off-the-shelf products or relying on generic solutions that claimed to work "for education" but were designed with one-size-fits-all thinking. We knew from experience that pre-packaged platforms often failed to account for the nuances of individual institutions, the quirks of legacy systems, the specific compliance obligations, or the culture and tone of a particular college.

Instead, we chose to engineer our own AI agents, in partnership with our consultants, so that every tool was designed with our systems, our people, and our strategic goals in mind. This approach gave us full control, not just over the features and user experience, but over the very logic, behaviour, and guardrails of the AI itself.

We were able to embed our own prompts, constraints, and safeguards in the back end, differentiating from agent to agent. We controlled the API endpoints, determined the datasets involved, and implemented filters that reflected our safeguarding policies and professional standards. We could decide, for instance, how the agent responded to uncertainty, when it should defer, what queries it should reject outright, and how to log and monitor interactions for transparency and improvement.

Equally important was our ability to tailor the language, tone, and purpose of each agent to reflect our college culture as well as the agent's purpose and audience. We didn't want cold, transactional tools, we wanted agents that felt human-centred, helpful, and embedded in the organisation's way of doing things. Whether responding to a staff query about a policy or supporting a student in navigating their timetable, every agent needed to speak with us, not at us.

And then there was data protection. The recurring theme here is that by developing tools within our own digital tenancy, we ensured that all AI usage remained compliant with GDPR, subject to internal governance, and aligned with our data minimisation and privacy standards. Sensitive information never left our ecosystem. We weren't at the mercy of commercial LLM data policies or unpredictable licence agreements. We were in the driving seat.

This bespoke development approach took more time and effort than a quick procurement route. But it paid dividends. It meant that every AI tool we rolled out had a clear rationale, a clear user base, and a clear governance structure behind it. They weren't experiments, they were solutions, designed to serve our community, support our goals, and evolve with us over time.

This phase of our journey wasn't just about building tools, it was about building capacity. We were learning how to design, test, refine, and govern AI within the fabric of our institution. We weren't just implementing AI; we were developing a model for how AI can be built responsibly and effectively within education, and how it can be shaped to serve, not steer, our values.

Understanding APIs: A Gateway to Bespoke AI Agents

An Application Programming Interface (API) is a structured way for different software applications to communicate with each other. In simple terms, it acts like a digital waiter: it takes requests from one system (like your AI agent), fetches the relevant data or service from another (like your MIS database), and returns the result. APIs are typically provided by platforms, tools, or services that offer specific functionality, such as AI models, data sources, payment systems, or communication tools, without exposing the complex inner workings.

When building tailored AI agents for a specific institution or use case, such as centralising all student support services like Student Buddy, APIs play a central role. They allow developers to:

- **Access advanced capabilities** without having to build everything from scratch (e.g., integrating ChatGPT, Google Gemini or Microsoft Azure AI services).
- **Pull real-time data** from internal systems or third-party platforms (e.g., a student's timetable from your MIS, their homework assignment details (from our enterprise software) or in our case, the timetable for the local bus company, which includes the College's services).
- **Ensure scalability** by distributing tasks and leveraging the computational power of cloud providers.
- **Maintain modularity**, making it easier to upgrade or replace individual components without rewriting the entire solution.

So, following the example of our AI digital assistant (chatbot) designed for students, it uses APIs to pull live timetable data, access test results, catering information, homework details, lesson resources, even bus timetables, as well as answer a range of questions around process and procedure.

Things to Consider When Using APIs

While APIs unlock powerful functionality, it's crucial to be mindful of several variables:

- **Terms and Conditions (T&Cs):** Each API comes with its own rules governing usage, data handling, privacy, and cost. Some impose strict rate limits, while others may restrict the type of content that can be processed or returned. Reviewing these terms is essential to ensure compliance, especially when dealing with sensitive educational data and students under 18.
- **Latency:** This refers to the time it takes for a request to be processed and a response returned. High latency can hinder the performance of real-time systems like chatbots or AI-powered tutors. Developers need to optimise response times and choose APIs with appropriate service levels.
- **Concurrency:** APIs vary in how many requests they can handle at the same time. A service with low concurrency limits may perform well under light use but struggle under the load of hundreds of simultaneous users. This is a key factor when deploying AI solutions at scale, particularly across entire student cohorts.
- **Response Detail:** Some APIs provide highly detailed outputs, such as full natural language explanations or structured data with confidence scores, while others return more basic or summarised information. Choosing the right level of detail depends on the application, whether it's generating feedback for students, analysing operational efficiency, or flagging potential risks (as mentioned in chapters 1 and 2).

APIs are the backbone of modern AI development, enabling bespoke agents to interact with the wider digital ecosystem. By understanding the technical and practical considerations, such as terms of use, latency, concurrency, and output detail, education leaders and developers can ensure their AI implementations are both effective and sustainable.

Our Initial Flagship Agents

Bespoke LLM

I have already introduced you to the agent at the heart of our AI ecosystem, Bespoke LLM: a secure, front-end to a large language model (LLM), developed entirely within our domain. More than just a technical tool, Bespoke LLM represented our strategic commitment to trust, safety, and long-term value for money in AI deployment. It was a carefully engineered solution, designed not only to perform, but to align with our institutional values, systems, and safeguarding responsibilities.

By building Bespoke LLM, we retained full control over its design, functionality, and data governance. allowing us to implement custom prompts and set clear usage boundaries. This ensured that staff could confidently input sensitive datasets, such as class-level attainment, behavioural notes, or internal documentation, knowing that all data remained securely within our digital tenancy and was fully compliant with GDPR. Crucially, unlike many commercial AI platforms, Bespoke LLM was configured not to train on user data, eliminating the risk of sensitive information being repurposed or accessed externally. This immediately established a foundation of trust with users, in the first instance, our staff, but eventually students (and their parents).

From the beginning, we built Bespoke LLM with student access in mind, not just staff. This required a far higher level of scrutiny and safeguarding. We embedded enhanced controls at every level of the system.

Unlike many commercial tools, Bespoke LLM was built to track and log both inputs and outputs (so both questions asked and answers given), allowing us to monitor usage patterns and ensure total transparency. This feature became a key part of our safeguarding and compliance framework. Every prompt submitted and every response given could be reviewed, enabling early identification of potential safeguarding or prevent concerns and triggering alerts if flagged terms were used.

To further strengthen safety, Bespoke LLM was configured to run behind our existing web filtering and monitoring systems, integrating seamlessly with our digital infrastructure. This meant the tool adhered to the same safeguarding expectations as every other college system, and its use could be governed by the same policies and oversight. Perhaps most importantly, it would flag any safeguarding concern or inappropriate use immediately.

This approach aligns closely with the Technology Acceptance Model (TAM), which identifies perceived usefulness and perceived ease of use as key enablers of adoption. Bespoke LLM was built to be both useful in solving real operational problems, and safe in how it handled data and user interaction. It also supported two critical aspects of Diffusion of Innovations Theory: trialability and observability. By allowing staff to experiment with Bespoke LLM in a low-risk, high-trust environment, and see immediate practical benefits, we created the conditions for deeper engagement and sustained use.

But what truly set Bespoke LLM apart was the comprehensive safeguarding framework built into its architecture. Recognising that we would eventually open up the tool to students, we went far beyond standard technical precautions. A number of advanced controls were embedded to protect users, especially younger learners, from inappropriate or potentially harmful outputs:

- Content filtering was built directly into the agent, preventing responses to queries on high-risk topics such as drug use, pornography, self-harm, or illegal activity.

- The agent ran behind our college-wide web filtering and monitoring system, ensuring it was subject to the same safeguarding oversight as all digital tools used in the institution.
- Every interaction, both input and output, was logged, allowing us to review usage, flag anomalies, and identify any safeguarding or prevent concerns in real time.
- If a prompt was deemed inappropriate or flagged by our filters, designated staff could be alerted through our safeguarding processes, ensuring timely human intervention if needed.
- A strict "100 per cent accuracy" threshold was enforced, meaning that if the model could not return a reliable, verified answer, it would say so clearly and confidently: "I am not able to answer that question." This not only reduced the risk of hallucinated outputs but also modelled responsible digital behaviour for students and staff alike.

This embedded caution reflected principles found in the Responsible Innovation theory (Stilgoe et al., 2013), which stresses the importance of anticipation, inclusion, reflexivity, and responsiveness when deploying emerging technologies. Our goal was not to build the most powerful tool, we wanted the most appropriate tool for our setting.

And while the safeguarding and technical controls made Bespoke LLM robust and compliant, our financial model made it sustainable. In future, rather than committing to costly commercial licences charged per user per month, Bespoke LLM operated on a usage-based, pay-as-you-go model. This offered significantly better value for money, allowing the college to scale AI usage gradually without locking itself into inflexible vendor agreements or high upfront costs. It also reduced our exposure to future pricing changes or access restrictions often imposed by proprietary platforms.

By combining strong pedagogy-informed design with robust ethical governance, Bespoke LLM became more than just a tool.

It became a trusted partner in our digital ecosystem, proving that AI in education doesn't have to come at the expense of safeguarding, autonomy, or affordability. Instead, when built with intention, it can amplify the best of what we already do, safely, ethically, and sustainably.

Student Buddy

Our second major development was Student Buddy, a student-facing digital assistant designed to provide round-the-clock support, guidance, and access to college services in a way that was intuitive, secure, and inclusive. While in the first instance, Bespoke LLM focused on empowering staff, Student Buddy was built to do the same for our learners, offering a smart, college-branded interface that brought together a wide range of services under one virtual roof. We know students won't log into various systems regularly or read frequent communications, instead they prefer to ask a question when the answer is pertinent to them. For example, students won't log into the college intranet each day to check the menus, they will ask a friend what their next lesson is, rather than log into the MIS/Timetable system.

Technically, Student Buddy was a significant achievement. Built on top of a LLM and again developed entirely within our digital tenancy, the agent leveraged the full power of the enterprise software ecosystem through API integrations. Student Buddy was able to pull information dynamically from across our entire software stack. But its true strength came from its integration with our Management Information System (MIS) and ability to read from our internal sites.

Using secure, role-based authentication tied to each student's login, Student Buddy retrieved personalised information from our MIS only relevant to the user accessing it. Timetables, exam schedules, attendance data, upcoming deadlines, live transport updates, and even bursary information could all be surfaced securely and contextually. This wasn't a static chatbot delivering generic responses, it was an intelligent assistant that provided each student with their information, in real time, and in a tone and format designed for them.

However, one of Student Buddy's most impactful features, its ability to read and retrieve content directly from our internal sites, allowing it to provide students with immediate, low-level health and well-being support, any time, day or night, and in complete confidence. By connecting to existing resources curated by our safeguarding and support teams, Student Buddy could signpost students to the right guidance without the need for them to search through multiple platforms or wait until college staff were available. Whether a student was feeling anxious, struggling with motivation, or just needed reassurance about where to turn, the agent offered a private, judgement-free way to access help, linking them to trusted internal materials, self-help strategies, and appropriate next steps, all within the safe boundaries of our college's digital ecosystem. This seamless access reinforced our wider commitment to proactive student support and digital inclusivity.

Security and privacy were paramount. Student Buddy authenticated every session via our single sign-on (SSO) and ensured that all MIS queries were scoped to that individual user's access rights. At no point could one student view another's data, and all interactions were monitored within our digital tenancy, making the agent fully GDPR-compliant. This careful architecture allowed us to unlock the value of personalisation without compromising on safety or integrity.

Student Buddy's development was also shaped by our commitment to accessibility and inclusion. The agent was built to be multilingual, with the ability to switch between languages on demand, particularly important for students with English as an additional language, or for communicating college information to families in our wider community. It included voice-to-text functionality, allowing students to interact with the tool using speech, and supported screen-reading technologies for visually impaired users. Users could toggle between dark and light modes, zoom in or out, or adjust settings to suit their preferences, ensuring the experience was as user-friendly as it was functional.

Perhaps most importantly, Student Buddy democratised access to information. Instead of needing to find the right member of staff, wait for office hours, or navigate multiple systems, students could get answers instantly, 24 hours a day, seven days a week, from a single, trusted source. Whether they needed help understanding the college's mobile phone policy, finding the contact details for the safeguarding team, or checking when the next bus was due to arrive, Student Buddy is their go-to digital companion.

By reducing the friction between questions and answers, Student Buddy empowered students to take greater ownership of their own learning, organisation, and well-being. And for staff, it reduced the burden of repeatedly fielding the same routine queries, freeing up time to focus on the kinds of support that require human presence and care.

What made Student Buddy exceptional was that it wasn't simply a chatbot bolted onto our systems; it was a fully integrated, student-centric information ecosystem, designed with purpose, built with trust, and delivered in a way that reflected our commitment to equity, personalisation, and digital maturity.

Back Office Agents: AI Agents That Transformed Our Operational Efficiency

Some of the most impactful tools we developed were also the most deceptively simple. While much of the national conversation around AI in education focused on teaching and learning, we recognised that the greatest immediate gains could be made by targeting the administrative backbone of the college, specifically, the repetitive, time-sensitive, error-prone processes that underpin student enrolment.

The following agents were among the first to be developed and deployed, and they quickly proved that targeted AI could transform high-volume workflows with measurable impact, improved accuracy, and better user experience, all while freeing staff to focus on work that requires human insight and care.

GCSE Results Agent

Every August, College and University enrolment teams across the UK face the high-pressure challenge of verifying student qualifications and manually entering results into Management Information Systems (MIS). It's a process that, while vital, is slow, labour-intensive, and prone to human error, especially when under pressure.

Our Results Agent changed this entirely. Students were invited to upload a photo of their results sheet via a secure interface on our application portal. The agent extracted the relevant data, in terms of subject, grade, and candidate details, using OCR (optical character recognition) and automatically populated the relevant fields in our MIS. Then on arrival at the College for the enrolment process, a quick human check was all that was needed.

The result was a huge efficiency gain. We saved over 93 labour hours during the face-to-face enrolment period alone, not to mention the huge number of hours avoided correcting the misspelt words like "Business" or "Religious", that often occur during the pressured process. So perhaps, more importantly, this agent improved accuracy and consistency, reducing the risk of data entry errors that could prevent a student accessing a certain programme of courses or later affect funding claims. For prospective students, it also streamlined the onboarding experience, replacing queues and paperwork with a seamless, person-focused interaction.

ID Checker

Verifying identity is another critical part of the application process, especially when it comes to ensuring compliance with legal and funding regulations. Traditionally, this has involved lengthy manual checks, cross-referencing multiple documents, and follow-up emails to clarify discrepancies.

The ID Checker Agent automated this process. Applicants were asked to upload a photo of a government-issued ID (e.g., passport or birth certificate). The agent cross-checked the key data points, including first name, surname, middle names, date of birth, and legal sex, against the information submitted in their application.

Where any mismatches occurred, the system automatically flagged them for review, ensuring that only legitimate applications progressed. This 100 per cent accuracy requirement was built into the prompts in the back end to ensure certainty. This agent not only protected data integrity and legal compliance for ILR (Individualised Learner Record) purposes, but it also saved a significant number of labour hours during the application window, something that it is hard to accurately estimate.

For applicants, it reduced delays and uncertainty. For staff, it eliminated one of the most repetitive and risk-laden manual processes in the system.

Photo Checker

While seemingly minor, collecting and verifying student ID photos is a notoriously frustrating task. Incorrect sizing, low-quality images, or failure to submit one altogether can create a backlog of administrative burden at the start of term, and delay ID card production.

The Photo Checker Agent was developed to streamline this process. Once a student uploaded their image, the agent automatically assessed it against college-specified criteria, checking image clarity, background uniformity, file type, face centring, and suitability for printing. If the image did not meet all the requirements, the system prompted staff to review the image.

This reduced the administrative load on staff, who no longer needed to manually review every submission, and ensured that photo ID cards could be processed and printed efficiently in bulk. While this may seem like a minor gain, it significantly improved the student welcome experience, again no queues, no last-minute photo booths, and no delays in accessing services.

Certificate AI

Once a student finishes their course, certificates begin arriving from a range of awarding bodies. These must be meticulously checked for accuracy in terms of names, subjects, grades, ULNs, and candidate numbers, all of which need to be verified and recorded. Previously, this was done by hand, one certificate at a time.

Certificate AI completely overhauled this process. Staff scanned the physical certificates, and the agent extracted the relevant information. It then checked that data against existing MIS records, flagged any discrepancies, and populated the certificate receipt date against each qualification on file. This was another example of the 100 per cent accuracy requirement being built in, in short it was either all correct or it was referred for human review.

This automation brought both speed and security. The agent ensured that no certificate went unlogged, and that every student's record was accurate and complete, critical for both compliance and student progression. It saved the college over 300 hours annually, and provided a clear audit trail for certificate management that was previously lacking.

Together, these four agents formed a group of intelligent assistants that quietly streamlined some of the most unglamorous, yet essential, parts of our college operations. They didn't make headlines, but they made a difference, to our staff capacity, our student experience, and our data accuracy.

These agents proved that small efficiencies, at scale, create transformation. They also validated our design principle: started with real problems, build targeted solutions, and keep people at the centre of the process. From here, the path to more ambitious AI applications became not only possible, but inevitable.

The Broader Agent Development and Ecosystem

By early 2025, we had developed a total of 15 bespoke AI agents with a further three having been commissioned. Each was created to address a specific operational challenge, to solve a specific problem or pinch point in processes.

Every AI agent we developed was subjected to a rigorous and methodical testing process before it ever reached a live environment. At the core of this was our use of a sandbox environment, a secure, isolated replica of our systems where agents could be trialled, tweaked, and stress-tested without any risk to real data, services, or users. It was here that we invited a diverse group of stakeholders to take on a critical role as part of our red team. Which of course made me "Red Team Leader" fulfilling one of my childhood (Star Wars related) dreams...

As previously mentioned, our red teams were made up of staff and when appropriate, students from across the college. Representatives from a cross-section of departments, roles, and digital confidence levels. They were tasked not just with using the tools, but with actively trying to break them. Their brief was clear: push each agent to its limits. Ask the awkward questions. Input deliberately confusing prompts. Look for errors, exploit vulnerabilities, and challenge assumptions. If something could go wrong, we wanted to find out in the sandbox, not in front of a live user.

This approach reflected principles from agile development and user-centred design, where feedback loops are continuous, fast, and grounded in real-world usage. But more than just a question-and-answer exercise, our red-teaming process became a powerful professional development tool.

For those staff involved, it demystified AI.

They weren't just passive recipients of new systems, they became co-creators, actively shaping how tools were developed and deployed. Through hands-on interaction, these staff gained first-hand insight into how AI agents worked, what their strengths and limitations were, and where guardrails needed to be built. Those involved quickly learned that AI is not infallible. It has boundaries. It needs prompting, context, and responsible framing. And most importantly, it performs best when paired with human judgement, not instead of it.

For many concerned, it was the first time they had been directly involved in developing digital tools. It built not only confidence but digital fluency, helping those staff become more comfortable with AI terminology, systems integration, data structures, and the ethical considerations underpinning its use. These insights were invaluable when it came time to roll the tools out more widely. Staff weren't just trained on the agents; they knew that other staff had helped train the agents through red-teaming.

Students, too, played a critical role. Their feedback helped uncover issues that adults might overlook, from unexpected phrasing and edge-case prompts to usability concerns around language, accessibility, or tone of voice. Involving students reinforced a key message: that these tools were being built with them, not for them. And their involvement gave us confidence that Bespoke LLM and Student Buddy were fit for purpose in a real educational context.

The red-teaming process also helped embed more of a culture of reflective innovation within the college. It modelled a way of working where it was safe to ask questions, safe to find flaws, and safe to say, "this isn't ready yet." That level of humility and honesty around technology is rare in education, and it became one of the benefits of our approach.

By treating red-teaming as both a technical safeguard and a learning opportunity, we not only improved the quality of our tools... we built trust. And in a sector where the fear of "getting it wrong" often stifles innovation, that trust was a powerful enabler of progress.

Inside-Out Innovation: The Strategic Advantages of Building Our Own AI Solutions

Our previously explained decision to build our own AI solutions, rather than purchasing off-the-shelf products, was the most pivotal choice we made. It wasn't just about functionality. It was about autonomy, alignment, and trust. This approach offered a number of critical advantages that went far beyond technical capability:

Customisation

Because we controlled the design and development process, we were able to shape each agent around the realities of our workflows, rather than contorting our processes to fit pre-built software. Whether it was automating result entry, checking ID documents, or providing 24/7 student support, each tool was tailored to reflect our systems, our language, our policies, and our culture. This meant we could create tools that genuinely worked for our people, with interfaces and logic grounded in how we already operated, rather than adopting generic, one-size-fits-all models.

Compliance

By building our AI agents within our digital tenancy, we ensured that all data processing remained fully under our control. This was critical in maintaining legal compliance and safeguarding sensitive information. Unlike commercial AI services that often store prompts and user data externally, sometimes even using them to train future models, our internal approach allowed us to manage exactly what data was accessed, how it was used, and who had oversight. This was especially important when handling student data, where even minor breaches could have major implications.

Cost Efficiency

As previously mentioned, commercial AI tools typically operate on per-user, per-month licence models, costs that scale rapidly and can become unsustainable for large institutions and unaffordable for others. By contrast, our model was built around API usage, meaning we only paid for what we actually used, measured in tokens. This pay-as-you-go structure allowed us to scale AI adoption in a way that was both flexible and financially sustainable without being tied to any one provider, Google, OpenAI, Microsoft. We weren't tied to restrictive vendor agreements, and we could manage costs based on real value delivered, not flat subscription fees.

Transparency and Accountability

One of the most significant benefits of bespoke development was the ability to log every query and every response. This created a full audit trail for each agent, ensuring that we could track usage patterns, evaluate tool performance, and investigate any concerns. This level of granular visibility simply isn't possible with most third-party systems. It gave our safeguarding and compliance teams the information they needed to feel confident, and provided a level of accountability that strengthened user trust.

Responsiveness and Agility

Owning the development pipeline meant we weren't reliant on external vendors for updates or fixes. When staff raised feedback, we could respond rapidly, refining prompts, improving logic, adjusting filters, or expanding capabilities without waiting on product roadmaps or update cycles. This created a culture of continuous improvement, where agents evolved based on real-world use and real user insight. AI wasn't something done to us, it was something built with us.

Ownership and Partnership

Perhaps most importantly, this approach fostered a deep sense of staff ownership amongst those involved. Because teams had been involved in testing, feedback, and even ideation, the tools weren't perceived as imposed innovations, they were shared successes. Lots of staff didn't just use the agents; they championed them. They could see their input reflected in the design, their challenges solved by the tools, and their values embedded in the functionality. This sense of partnership wasn't incidental; it was essential to our change management strategy, and it became one of the most powerful enablers of adoption.

By taking this inside-out approach, we gained more than just customised AI, we gained clarity, control, and cultural alignment. We de-risked our digital transformation by building on our own terms, at our own pace, and always with our community at the centre. In doing so, we laid the foundation not just for innovation, but for sustainable, values-driven change.

Engineering Trust and Capability

As AI agents became more embedded in college life, we made a concerted effort to build trust. This meant being honest about what AI could and couldn't do. It meant setting guardrails, like the accuracy threshold, and providing clear training.

It also meant acknowledging and correcting misunderstandings with stakeholders. For instance, many students assumed Student Buddy was a full LLM with internet access, rather than a digital assistant with access to a limited knowledge base. Through ongoing dialogue and structured learning, we helped build AI understanding and literacy across our community.

This chapter in our journey wasn't just about building software. It was about building confidence, capacity, and credibility, three ingredients essential for sustained innovation.

With the agents in place and adoption growing, our attention turned to the bigger picture. What challenges did we face, and how could we overcome them while maintaining momentum?

Conclusion: Building with Purpose, Scaling with Confidence

Chapter 3 was more than a technical milestone in our journey. It marked the moment where vision became visible. Where abstract ambition was translated into functioning tools. And where a college didn't just adopt AI, it authored it.

By choosing to build from the inside out, we didn't just create bespoke agents, we cultivated a model of intentional innovation. One where control, context, and care mattered as much as code. One where the "how" was as important as the "what".

Our agents weren't off-the-shelf solutions dropped into an unfamiliar landscape. They were designed with, and for, our community. Shaped by the people who knew the work, governed by the principles that defined our culture, and engineered to solve problems we had mapped with precision.

We built slowly. Deliberately. Safely. We tested rigorously, involved our staff deeply, and never let hype outpace honesty. That pace allowed us to make smarter choices, not just about tools, but about trust, ethics, and long-term sustainability.

And while the chapter closes with functional agents like Bespoke LLM and Student Buddy, it also signals the emergence of something even more valuable: internal capability. We weren't just building products; we were building people. A group of staff who could prompt, query, challenge, and refine. A group of students who could test, critique, and shape their own digital experiences. Leaders who could see AI not as a threat to be managed, but as a platform for transformation.

In short, we built from the inside out, and in doing so, we laid the blueprint for what came next: scaling that wasn't rushed but rooted. Not growth for growth's sake, but growth with clarity, compassion, and purpose.

The next chapter? It's about that very scaling. About ensuring that what worked in pockets can work at pace. And that our values, so carefully embedded at the start, remain the thread that binds every step forward.

> **Chapter 3: 🎨 What We Learned**
>
> - In-house, bespoke AI agents offer flexibility, data security, and alignment with local values.
> - Control over development allows for guardrails, safeguarding filters, and modular scaling.
> - Building internally reduces long-term dependency on vendors and costly licences.
> - Developing AI is not just about tech, it's about capacity, governance, and cross-functional learning.
>
> **Chapter 3: 💡 Key Reflection Questions**
>
> - Are you prioritising internal development of AI tools to ensure control, customisation, and cost-efficiency?
> - What criteria are you using to decide which AI agents to build first?
> - How are you ensuring that each AI tool directly addresses a specific operational need?
> - Are your AI agents designed with built-in safeguards, such as confidence thresholds and response logging?
> - How are you balancing innovation with user confidence, testing each tool before scaling?
> - Do your AI tools operate within your secure digital tenancy, and are they compliant by design?
> - How are students and staff involved in red-teaming and stress-testing your AI agents?
> - Are your early AI builds generating measurable value and building internal belief in the long-term strategy?

CHAPTER 4: OVERCOMING CHALLENGES AND MANAGING RISKS

The implementation of artificial intelligence-based solutions was never assumed to be straightforward. From the outset, we understood that integrating a new and rapidly evolving technology into a complex, people-centred educational environment would come with significant risks, uncertainties, and operational challenges. But we also knew something else, something crucial: avoiding those risks entirely would mean standing still. And standing still, in a sector facing rising expectations, constrained budgets, and relentless performance demands, was not a sustainable option.

In this sense, our approach echoed the core principles of Kotter's Change Model (1996), which begins with the urgent need to establish a compelling reason for change. For us, that urgency was clear: workload was rising, support structures were under strain, and legacy systems were no longer fit for purpose. The case for doing nothing had collapsed under its own weight.

Still, acknowledging the need for change is only the beginning. What followed was not a linear journey, nor a frictionless one. It was a deliberate, values-led process, one rooted in humility, collaboration, and the understanding that innovation is as much about culture as it is about code. We embraced ambiguity, learned from missteps, and remained open to feedback throughout.

As mentioned previously, at the heart of our strategy was a firm belief that AI must serve people, not the other way around. This conviction aligns closely with the idea of technological humanism

(Feenberg, 1991), which argues that technology must be shaped by human values and institutions, not imposed upon them. I have made it clear that we weren't interested in deploying AI simply because it was available or fashionable. We were interested in deploying it responsibly, transparently, and inclusively, to improve work lives and support the mission of education.

Throughout this journey, we also leaned on the idea of psychological safety (Edmondson, 1999), creating an environment where staff could ask difficult questions, admit uncertainty, and share critical feedback without fear of reprisal. This was vital when dealing with a new and often misunderstood technology like AI. Trust was the soil in which our innovation had to grow.

Ultimately, this chapter explores not just the challenges we faced, but the approach we took to overcome them. An approach grounded in inclusion over imposition, dialogue over decree, and learning over perfection. The result was not a flawless rollout, but a deeply human one, where mistakes were expected, successes were shared, and every step forward was guided by our belief in responsible innovation.

Navigating the Complexity of Early Adoption

Being early adopters meant forging a path without a map. We stepped into uncharted territory, where case studies were scarce, best practices were still forming, and there was little consistency in the tools, standards, or support available across the sector. It was, in many ways, a classic example of Rogers' Diffusion of Innovations theory (2003), which identifies early adopters as those who are willing to tolerate uncertainty, experiment ahead of the curve, and lead change before widespread validation exists. In this space, we were not following precedent, we were helping to set it.

At times, the journey was exhilarating but lonely. We could feel the energy of possibility, the momentum of change. But at other times, it was daunting. We faced a perfect storm of strategic, technical, cultural, and operational challenges, often simultaneously, with little in terms of guidance or support available to us. Tools didn't always work as intended. Timelines slipped. Feedback forced us to revisit earlier decisions. Occasionally, agents that once seemed like strong bets were rendered obsolete overnight by the astonishing pace of advancement in commercial LLMs. The rug could be pulled out from under us not by error, but by innovation itself.

And yet, we continued. Because we knew that risk is not the opposite of progress, it is its companion. This echoes the sentiment in Heifetz and Linsky's Adaptive Leadership theory (2002), which argues that leading through complex, adaptive change requires distinguishing between technical challenges (solvable with known processes) and adaptive challenges (which require learning, experimentation, and shifts in mindset). Implementing AI was firmly in the latter category. There was no playbook, only our values, our people, and our willingness to learn as we went with the support of our consultants.

Crucially, we were supported by a leadership that valued psychological safety (Edmondson, 1999). The early reassurance that some of what we built would fail, and that this would not be seen as failure, gave me the freedom to try. This was not innovation built on fear of getting it wrong, but on confidence that mistakes were part of the process. It shifted our mindset from risk-averse to risk-aware, where the goal was not to eliminate all uncertainty, but to navigate it responsibly.

This mindset allowed us to operate with an element of confidence, but aware enough to course-correct if needed. We also had a better understanding of what to expect and the challenges that we faced. This made it easier for us to abandon ideas or developments that didn't deliver, and to share our learning openly so that others could build upon it. In doing so, we didn't just adopt AI, we helped model a way to do it well, in the absence of guarantees, and in the presence of real, human complexity. At this time,

I found real value and comfort in having a team around me that questioned, challenged and debated our steps. This meant we were always looking for the best solution rather than the quickest or easiest.

Agreeing Priorities and Defining Outcomes

AI generated genuine excitement across sections of our college. There was a palpable sense that something new, something powerful, was becoming possible. But with that excitement came a different kind of challenge: uncertainty. Different teams, or even individuals within the teams, imagined different futures. For some, AI meant intelligent automation of administrative work; for others, it meant new pedagogical tools or enhanced student support. What quickly became clear was that not everyone could articulate exactly what they wanted, only that what they had wasn't working.

This echoes Ackoff's (1974) distinction between messes and problems. A problem, he argued, is something with clear boundaries and a known solution pathway. A mess, by contrast, is a complex, interrelated set of issues that defy straightforward definition. The early stages of our AI journey were not about solving problems. They were about untangling a mess of assumptions, expectations, frustrations, and hopes.

We soon realised that our biggest early challenge wasn't technical, it was aligning purpose. Without shared understanding, even the most capable tools risked being underused, misused, or resisted. So, we deliberately slowed the pace and returned to the basics. We asked:

- What are we actually trying to solve?
- Who benefits?
- How will we know if it's working?

This approach mirrored principles from logic modelling and theory of change frameworks, which emphasise working backwards from desired outcomes to define actions, inputs, and success metrics. It helped us move from excitement to intentionality, from vague ambition to focused, achievable objectives.

We also grounded this process in the principles of co-design (Sanders & Stappers, 2008), involving staff and students not just as end users, but as co-creators of the AI agents being developed. Through workshops, sandbox testing, and open feedback loops, we created a culture where everyone's voice could shape the direction of innovation. This helped us avoid the pitfall of technological determinism, where tools are imposed top-down without regard for local context or human factors.

Crucially, we developed a shared language of outcomes. By focusing conversations on what success would look and feel like, rather than what the tool should do, we unlocked new clarity. Different teams might not have known which features they needed, but they could describe the pain points, inefficiencies, or missed opportunities they experienced daily. That became our design brief.

In doing so, we shifted the conversation from tools to transformation, from implementing AI for its own sake to implementing it with purpose. This not only improved the quality of what we built, it deepened trust, strengthened collaboration, and ensured that innovation was grounded in real need, not hypothetical capability.

Managing the Cost of Innovation

Innovation, especially when it is bespoke, intentional, and values-driven, doesn't come cheap. While our approach deliberately steered us away from costly SaaS subscriptions that compound over time, the reality was that building our own AI ecosystem demanded significant upfront investment. We had to commit resources to expert consultancy, cloud infrastructure, staff time, and capability development, all at a time when funding in the further education sector was already under pressure.

To manage this challenge, we applied a strategic principle common in project portfolio management theory (Archer & Ghasemzadeh, 1999): we prioritised early, high-impact deliverables. By focusing first on agents with clear, measurable returns, those which saved hours of manual processing, we created internal momentum and external proof of value. These time savings weren't just impressive on paper; they allowed us to reinvest capacity back into the programme, creating a self-sustaining cycle of incremental innovation.

This phased, feedback-driven approach also aligns with Lean Start-up Methodology (Ries, 2011), particularly the idea of building a "Minimum Viable Product" (MVP) that can be tested, validated, and iterated upon before scaling further. We weren't trying to launch the perfect tool first time, we were trying to learn, refine, and build tools that met the evolving needs of our college. That mindset was vital because being first meant being vulnerable to rapid obsolescence.

In some cases, a feature we had invested in turned out to be unstable or poorly documented, given the immaturity of many commercial LLM platforms. In others, a better tool arrived weeks after we had deployed our own, rendering our solution technically inferior but still strategically informative. These moments were frustrating, and to me at the time, felt like failure – but they were also deeply educational. I was very much learning as I went in terms of this emerging technology and its capabilities.

Here, Argyris's concept of double-loop learning (1977) becomes relevant. Rather than treating unexpected or disappointing outcomes as isolated failures, we viewed them as opportunities to revisit and question our core assumptions. What did this experience reveal about our decision-making? How could it reshape our development process? This type of reflective practice allowed us to embed organisational learning, rather than merely fixing technical issues.

As one of the first colleges in the country to build AI agents at this depth and scale, we carried that weight knowingly. But we also recognised that the cost of waiting would be even greater, lost time, continued inefficiencies, and missed opportunities to develop institutional knowledge in an emerging field.

Ultimately, even when specific outcomes were limited, the learning was invaluable. We gained insight into our infrastructure, our workflows, our culture, and our staff capacity. We improved our digital strategy, our internal data handling, and our approach to cross-team collaboration. These weren't incidental side effects; they were the building blocks of a system ready to embrace the next wave of innovation with greater agility and wisdom.

Managing Expectations and Avoiding the Hype

As I mentioned, we were clear from the beginning: AI is not a silver bullet. It cannot, and should not, replace the human relationships that sit at the heart of education. No algorithm can replicate the emotional intelligence of a teacher, the pastoral insight of a tutor, or the intuition of a support worker who notices when something just isn't right. But clarity in principle doesn't always translate into shared understanding, especially in the context of widespread technological hype.

The media landscape surrounding AI, particularly LLMs, has created a fertile ground for misconceptions and extremes. Some staff believed that AI would soon be able to mark essays, design entire lesson plans, and automate behaviour management. Others worried it would de-skill their roles or eventually make them redundant. These diverging expectations created a kind of cognitive dissonance, heightened by the speed at which AI tools were being adopted and talked about outside of the classroom.

This phenomenon is well captured by Rogers' Diffusion of Innovations Theory (2003), which categorises adopters based on their readiness for change and their perception of risk. Early adopters within our college (like me) were enthusiastic but sometimes overzealous, while more cautious colleagues expressed legitimate concerns about automation and job security. Left unmanaged, this divergence could have fractured the implementation effort. The key, as Rogers suggests, was to support progression through the innovation-decision process: from awareness and persuasion through to decision, implementation, and confirmation.

To navigate this tension, we focused heavily on communication and transparency. We held staff briefings, sent communications, answered questions and held discussions, ensuring that no question was off limits and that both enthusiasm and scepticism were welcomed. We shared plans, clarified timelines, and were honest about what our agents could and could not do. We avoided hyperbole and instead rooted our messaging in real examples of workload reduction, improved accuracy, and enhanced student experience. All this whilst continually reassuring staff that this was not about reducing the number of staff employed, but to create more capacity to cope with the growing demands.

This commitment to honest, inclusive dialogue reflects the principles of transformational leadership (Bass & Avolio, 1994), particularly the emphasis on individualised consideration and intellectual stimulation. We encouraged staff to ask questions, challenge assumptions, and see themselves as co-creators of our AI systems. This helped shift the narrative from "Will AI replace me?" to "How can AI support me?"

Our implementation model was also iterative by design, reflecting principles from Agile development and the Lean Start-up methodology (Ries, 2011). Rather than aiming for a fully-fledged rollout, we launched in phases, treating each agent as a working prototype that could be refined over time. This approach allowed us to under-promise and over-deliver, earning trust incrementally rather than demanding it up front.

In doing so, we began to build trust, not just tools or agents. Trust that these systems were designed to support people, not replace them. Trust that feedback would be listened to. Trust that mistakes wouldn't be hidden but shared and learned from. This trust was not an accidental by-product, it was the core infrastructure of our AI deployment.

As Edmondson (1999) highlights in her work on psychological safety, environments where people feel safe to ask questions, admit gaps in knowledge, and raise concerns without fear of reprisal are the ones most likely to foster sustainable innovation. That's what we aimed to build. A college culture where technology was seen not as a threat or saviour, but as a tool, one that is only ever as effective as the human insight, care, and collaboration that surround it.

Ethical, Technical, and Cultural Risks

The ethical implications of AI in education are both complex and unavoidable. While AI presents transformative opportunities, it also introduces a new class of risks, some technical, others philosophical, that challenge our established norms around fairness, consent, professionalism, and pedagogical integrity. We made a deliberate choice to confront these issues early and openly. We recognised that ethics couldn't be treated as a "bolt-on" to innovation; they had to be baked into the design, deployment, and governance of every agent we created.

In doing so, we aligned with the principles of Responsible Research and Innovation (RRI) (Stilgoe, Owen, & Macnaghten, 2013), which emphasise anticipation, reflexivity, inclusion, and responsiveness. We understood that responsible AI is not just about what a system can do, but about what it should do, for whom, under what conditions, and with what consequences.

We faced challenges in seven key areas:

Bias and Fairness

AI models, particularly LLMs, are trained on vast datasets pulled from across the internet, datasets that inevitably contain historical, cultural, and structural biases. Without careful design, these biases can be baked into AI outputs, reinforcing existing inequalities.

We sought to limit this risk in several ways. We kept all agent development within our tenancy, where we could control data flow and configuration. We applied strict prompt engineering in the construction of the agents to reduce ambiguity and prevent unwanted outputs. Most importantly, we implemented a "100 per cent accuracy or do not answer" policy into many of our agents, ensuring agents would withhold responses if the risk of misinformation or inappropriate interpretation was too high.

This feature became a central part of our ethical risk management, reducing hallucinations, protecting users, and modelling responsible use of AI.

Transparency and Accountability

One of the most pressing concerns in AI ethics is the "black box" nature of many systems. Users are often left in the dark about how decisions are made, what data is being used, and whether outputs are trustworthy. This erodes accountability, particularly in sensitive educational contexts where decisions impact safeguarding, well-being, and attainment.

To counter this, we ensured that every query made to our agents, and every AI-generated response, was logged and auditable. This supported transparency, enabled retrospective analysis, and created a safety net for safeguarding monitoring. Our approach reflected principles from Floridi and Cowls' AI Ethics Framework (2019), particularly their emphasis on explainability and auditability as prerequisites for just and accountable AI.

Consent and Safeguarding

In an educational setting, the ethical use of AI intersects directly with legal responsibilities around data protection and child safety. For students under the age of 18, obtaining informed parental consent was not just a policy requirement, it was a moral imperative.

We developed a robust process for collecting, managing, and applying consent data. Integrated into our MIS and our agent access controls, this system ensured that only students with appropriate consent could access AI tools, and only in ways that were appropriate to their needs. This mirrors the principle of data minimisation outlined in GDPR legislation and reinforced by ethical guidelines from the Information Commissioner's Office (ICO).

Though slow to implement effectively, this process strengthened the culture of trust and compliance around our deployment.

AI Literacy

A recurring challenge was the widespread conflation of all AI tools with the likes of SnapAI or ChatGPT. This blurred understanding of what AI could and couldn't do and created both false expectations and misplaced concerns. Some staff and students thought that all our tools could browse the internet or generate images. Others were unaware of the structured constraints and internal safeguards we had put in place.

In line with Tambe et al.'s (2019) call for "AI readiness" in organisations, we treated each launch, particularly Student Buddy, as a teachable moment. We created video's that demystified the technology, clarified functionality, and addressed misconceptions. This effort was the start of what would become our broader AI literacy strategy. Aimed not only to improve digital capability, but to empower users to engage critically and ethically with these new tools.

Pedagogical Concerns

AI's entry into the classroom prompted deeper philosophical questions about the nature of teaching, learning, and authentic student engagement. There was a risk, well recognised in educational literature, that poorly implemented AI could lead to over-reliance, undermining critical thinking, student voice, and teacher agency. However, to coin a phrase: "AI is already out of the box". The technology is here and clearly being used by some staff and students, whether we like it or not!

Therefore, we framed AI not as a substitute for existing teaching practice, but as a potential for augmentation or redefinition. Staff were encouraged to use AI to reduce admin, spark creativity, or provide differentiated support, but not to offload responsibility or diminish human interaction.

Equally, students were beginning to be taught to see AI outputs as starting points for analysis, not definitive answers. This helped maintain the role of human judgement at the centre of learning, where students actively engage in meaning-making rather than passively consuming content.

Data Privacy and Security

Given the sensitivity of educational data, security was non-negotiable. Every agent underwent a Data Protection Impact Assessment (DPIA) and was reviewed by our internal Data Protection Officer. Agents were housed in our digital domain, operated only within approved parameters, and were deliberately restricted in functionality (e.g. no images or videos) to prevent misuse.

As we navigated the risks inherent in early AI adoption, it became increasingly clear that technical safeguards alone were not enough. We needed to view our agent deployments through the wider lens of agent governance. Recent emerging research, such as the comprehensive *Agent Governance: A Field Guide* (2025), echo that approach, it proposes a taxonomy of interventions, covering alignment, control, visibility, and societal integration, which aim to ensure agents behave in ways consistent with human values, operate within clear constraints, and remain observable and secure. While our local context focuses on education, the principles of rollback infrastructure, activity logging, and equitable access speak directly to the systems we must build today to safeguard the futures we cannot yet predict. Adopting these principles, even in an adapted form, can help educational institutions avoid downstream risks while building public trust in AI deployments.

Understanding AI Hallucinations and Their Value in the Right Situations

One of the most widely discussed limitations of generative AI models, especially LLMs like ChatGPT, is their tendency to "hallucinate." In simple terms, hallucination refers to the AI generating content that sounds plausible but is factually incorrect, fabricated, or ungrounded in the training data. This might be a misquoted statistic, a made-up reference, or an imaginary policy that doesn't exist.

To leaders and professionals in education, this can understandably raise red flags. After all, accuracy is vital in strategic planning, safeguarding, curriculum development, and policy decisions. Yet, as with any limitation, understanding the root of the issue reveals a more nuanced reality, and even opens the door to creative possibilities.

Why Do Hallucinations Happen?

LLMs generate text by predicting the most likely sequence of words based on patterns in vast amounts of data. They do not "know" facts in the way a human does, nor do they verify information unless explicitly programmed or connected to a reliable data source. In the absence of clear guidance or when operating in ambiguous or highly novel contexts, the model may default to creative synthesis; essentially, generating something that "sounds right" based on what it's seen before.

This is not due to a fault in the technology, but rather a consequence of how these models are designed: to be fluent, not factual.

When Hallucinations Are Problematic

In decision-making contexts that rely on hard data, such as financial forecasting, policy analysis, or health and safety compliance, hallucinations must be identified and controlled. Relying on false outputs in these areas could lead to misguided investments, reputational risks, or even legal implications. Here, using AI tools with embedded fact-checking, audit trails, or connections to trusted databases is essential.

But Here's the Twist: Hallucinations Can Be Helpful

Despite the name, hallucinations are not always useless. In creative or speculative contexts, they can be incredibly valuable. Consider these examples:

- **Strategic Planning Exercises:** When brainstorming future scenarios, AI-generated "hallucinations" can surface novel ideas that might not have emerged through traditional planning. They can simulate possible futures, playing out "what if" scenarios to support blue-sky thinking.
- **Proposal Writing and Drafting:** If you're generating the first draft of a report, AI may introduce unconventional suggestions that, while not strictly accurate, prompt new lines of inquiry or uncover blind spots in your planning.
- **Training Materials:** AI might produce varied, even fictionalised, case studies or role-play scenarios for training purposes. While not "real," these can enrich professional development resources and stimulate critical thinking.

- **Inspirational Leadership Communication:** When crafting speeches or vision statements, the richness of AI-generated language, even when loosely grounded, can help shape a compelling narrative or reframe institutional challenges in engaging ways.

Managing Hallucinations Responsibly

Recognising the dual nature of hallucinations, limitation and opportunity, is crucial. To harness their value safely:

- **Clearly define the task:** Use precise prompts and provide context to minimise ambiguity.
- **Fact-check where necessary:** Always verify outputs when working with data, policy, or public communications.
- **Use hallucinations as a starting point:** Treat AI outputs as drafts, not final products.
- **Build awareness in your teams:** Help colleagues understand the limitations of generative tools so that hallucinations don't slip through unnoticed.

In essence, hallucinations reflect the model's ability to extrapolate and imagine. When used in the right context, with human oversight, they can become a surprising source of innovation in our educational leadership toolkit.

Practical Implementation Barriers

Cost and Resourcing: Navigating the Realities of Innovation

One of the more tangible challenges of implementing bespoke AI solutions in education was the issue of cost and resourcing. Innovation is often portrayed as sleek and seamless, but the reality, particularly for early adopters, is that it is resource-intensive, iterative, and, as I found, at times exhausting.

While we deliberately avoided the long-term financial burden of per-user SaaS licences, the short-term costs of bespoke development, consultancy, training, infrastructure, and time were substantial. This is a well-documented pattern in innovation strategy, reflected in Christensen's theory of disruptive innovation (1997), which highlights that early-stage disruption often requires disproportionate investment without immediate returns.

To manage this as much as possible, we started with low-complexity, high-impact use cases as previously explained, where the benefits were tangible and measurable. These early wins created a "proof of concept" effect that helped secure internal support and justify further investment. In essence, we were building our innovation capability incrementally, reinvesting time and trust as much as financial savings.

The resource intensity of the early months, from discovery workshops to red-team testing, from prompt engineering to policy development, demanded cross-functional collaboration at an unprecedented level. It wasn't just about funding; it was about staff availability, technical skills, leadership bandwidth, and emotional energy. This aligns with Fullan's theory of educational change (2007), which reminds us that large-scale change is always as much about human capacity as it is about structural reform.

Complex Use Cases: The Limits of Early AI

Some operational areas, however, were not suitable for automation, at least in the short term. A notable example was timetabling, where the number of interdependencies, conditional rules, and site-specific nuances quickly overwhelmed the capabilities of early-stage LLM agents. These use cases highlighted a vital distinction in the AI space: not all problems are ready for automated solutions.

In these instances, we embraced the idea that decision-makers must work within the constraints of the information, technology, and resources available to them. Rather than force-fit a solution, we paused development in these areas, reflected on the complexity, and explored hybrid human-AI approaches instead.

For example, we shifted focus from fully automating timetable construction to developing an agent that could support the process by timetabling our music tuition lessons, retrieving room availability data, flagging staff clashes, or visualising alternatives based on staff input.

Acknowledging these limits didn't feel like failure, it felt like maturity. It reinforced a critical part of our AI philosophy: that innovation should serve the system, not overwhelm it. And it taught us that the art of AI implementation lies not just in technical brilliance, but in knowing when to stop, pivot, or adapt.

Taken together, our approach to cost and complexity demonstrated a commitment to strategic patience, balancing ambition with realism, investment with reflection. It ensured that we didn't just build tools, but built a model for sustainable innovation, one that could scale, flex, and learn as fast as the technology itself.

Digital Equity: Bridging the Divide in a Rapidly Advancing World

Digital equity is no longer a "nice to have", it is a foundational requirement for educational and operational success in the 21st century. As technology continues to evolve at pace, the digital divide is no longer a simple matter of who has a laptop and who doesn't. It now spans access to powerful tools like LLMs, quality internet access, and the core skills needed to thrive in a tech-enabled environment.

At the most basic level, digital equity starts with access to suitable devices and reliable connectivity. Lessons learned during the COVID 19 pandemic taught us that inconsistent access to a laptop or tablet, or even relying on a shared device at home, severely limits a student's ability to engage meaningfully with learning platforms, research, independent study, or remote support. Mobile phones, though widely owned, are not a substitute for a full-function device when it comes to completing coursework, developing digital skills, or engaging with more sophisticated tools such as coding platforms, data analysis software, or generative AI tools. Likewise, without high-speed and stable internet access, even the best devices are rendered ineffective.

Rethinking Digital Literacy: Beyond the "Digital Native" Myth

We often assume that today's learners are inherently digitally literate, after all, they live on their phones. But that assumption can be dangerously misleading. Comfort with social media apps does not equate to capability in digital communication, productivity tools, or safe and effective use of AI. Many students cannot write a formal email, format a document, or navigate file storage systems, all critical skills for further education and the workplace. This disconnect highlights the need for intentional, structured digital literacy education. Without it, we risk setting students up to fall behind in a world that demands far more than scrolling and swiping.

Understanding and Accessing AI: A New Frontier

The rise of AI adds a new dimension to digital equity. For many students, their understanding of artificial intelligence is confined to consumer-facing tools like Snap AI, Meta AI, or ChatGPT, often experienced through casual use, not structured learning. As LLMs become embedded in productivity suites, research tools, and administrative systems, the gap between those who can leverage AI meaningfully and those who cannot will only widen.

It is not enough to introduce students to AI, we must ensure they have equitable access to premium-level LLMs that are safe, powerful, and capable of enhancing their learning and creativity. This includes access through institutional subscriptions or managed platforms, rather than leaving students reliant on limited free versions or excluding them entirely from these tools. Without equal access, AI becomes another tool of exclusion, not empowerment.

The Risk of a Digital Chasm

Digital equity is not achieved by ticking a box. It requires deliberate focus across four pillars:

1. Access to suitable devices
2. Reliable connectivity
3. Strong digital literacy
4. Equitable access to premium AI tools

Without all four, the digital divide becomes a chasm. One that separates those who are equipped for a tech-augmented world from those who are left behind, not because of lack of potential, but because of lack of access.

As educational leaders, we have a responsibility to bridge that chasm. Not only for the benefit of our students, but for the health and future of our institutions and society at large.

Conclusion: Courage, Clarity and the Willingness to Learn

For us, the implementation of artificial intelligence was never a question of if, it was a question of how. And as this chapter has shown, that "how" demanded more than technical know-how or project planning. It required courage. Clarity of vision. Deep listening. And above all, a willingness to lead with values in a domain often dominated by hype.

We entered this work not as passive adopters, but as active shapers, fully aware that the road ahead was uncharted, and that the tools we were building might soon be outpaced by the very technology we were trying to harness. But in choosing to move forward anyway, we modelled what Heifetz and Linsky (2002) call adaptive leadership, the ability to mobilise people through uncertainty, not around it.

What emerged was not a flawless model, but a mature, reflective, and deeply human approach to innovation. One where challenges were expected, and where ethical tensions, technical setbacks, and cultural hesitations were not seen as barriers to progress, but as essential components of it. We didn't avoid risk; we managed it responsibly. And in doing so, we moved from reactive implementation to proactive design.

Through co-design, transparency, and continuous communication, we cultivated psychological safety (Edmondson, 1999), enabling our staff to explore new tools without fear of judgement. Through prioritised development and iterative rollouts, we adopted the spirit of Lean Start-up thinking (Ries, 2011), allowing us to learn fast, fail safely, and reinvest quickly. And through a commitment to Responsible Research and Innovation (Stilgoe et al., 2013), we ensured that our AI systems were not just efficient, but just, inclusive, and accountable.

This chapter has shown that innovation in education is never just about the technology, it is about people, systems, relationships, and trust. It is about balancing ambition with humility, vision with practicality, and speed with care. The challenges we encountered, and continue to encounter, have made us better leaders, better collaborators, and better custodians of the tools we build.

In the end, our most powerful learning was this: Innovation is not the absence of difficulty, but the presence of intent. With that intent firmly grounded in our mission, and with a growing ecosystem of trust, clarity, and capability, we emerged from this chapter of our journey not just with agents, dashboards, or policies, but with a culture of responsible innovation, ready to evolve as the technology does.

The work ahead remains complex. But the foundations are strong. And in the chapters that follow, we begin to move from infrastructure to impact, from building tools to transforming experiences for staff and students alike.

Chapter 4: 🧠 What We Learned

- Risk isn't a reason to avoid AI, it's a reason to lead it responsibly.
- Psychological safety and permission to fail are essential for innovation.
- Hallucinations and inaccuracies can be managed with the right constraints and design logic.
- Trust is earned through transparency, red-teaming, and visible commitment to ethics.

Chapter 4: 💡 Key Reflection Questions

- What are the biggest cultural, ethical, or technical risks associated with AI in your institution?
- How are you managing expectations around what AI can and cannot do at this stage?
- Do you have a clear plan for prioritising high-impact, low-risk use cases before attempting complex builds?
- How are you addressing the financial implications of innovation, both upfront and ongoing?
- What's your strategy for responding to AI hallucinations or errors in a way that maintains trust?
- Are your systems and processes designed to identify and mitigate safeguarding concerns in AI use?
- How are you bridging the digital divide to ensure equitable access to AI tools across your institution?
- Are you building the capacity, in terms of skills, systems, and mindset, to adapt to fast-moving technology?

CHAPTER 5: UNLOCKING THE BENEFITS OF AI IN EDUCATION

With the foundations laid and the risks responsibly navigated, our focus began to shift from building the agents to realising their value. What had once been a bold vision and carefully managed implementation effort was now entering a new phase: one where artificial intelligence was no longer discussed in abstract terms but experienced daily by staff and students. The theoretical had become practical. The experimental had become operational. AI was no longer an emerging concept; it was a lived, and soon to be embedded part of college life.

This chapter marks a deliberate turning point in our journey, from implementation to impact. It is where strategy meets culture, and where the tools we had so carefully developed began to generate outcomes that went beyond the spreadsheet. These were not just time savings or workflow automations. They were changes in confidence, capacity, access, and inclusion. They were improvements in well-being, responsiveness, and resilience. And they weren't happening *to* the college, they were being shaped by it.

As Fullan (2001) reminds us in his work on deep change in education, true innovation occurs not when systems are replaced, but when values and behaviours shift. That's what began to happen here. Our approach, grounded in purpose, trust, and co-design, began to unlock real-world advantages, not only for those who had led the work, but for those who would now engage with it, even those who had once been sceptical of it.

What follows is a closer look at those benefits: how they emerged, what they meant, and why they mattered. In doing so, we reflect not only on what AI gave us, but on what it revealed about the power of inclusive, values-led digital transformation in education.

From Efficiency to Empowerment

One of the most immediate and impactful benefits we observed from the deployment of certain AI agents was their dramatic increase in operational efficiency of the tasks that they addressed. Although just marginal gains in terms of the whole organisation. This was now about reimagining how core college functions were executed, removing bottlenecks, reducing duplication, and enabling staff to spend their time where it mattered most.

Take Certificate AI, for example. In automating the process of validating and matching thousands of incoming qualification results against our internal systems, it saved the equivalent of over 300 staff hours per year. This was not just an optimisation, to those staff affected, it was a transformation. Previously, this process required sustained concentration, spreadsheet juggling, and manual verification that inevitably carried risk and absorbed valuable staff resources during one of the most critical points in the academic calendar. With Certificate AI, those tasks were completed rapidly, accurately, and consistently. Yes, across our organisation, 300 labour hours is nothing, but 10 of these solutions? 20?

As Hammer and Champy (1993) argued in their foundational work on business process reengineering, the role of technology is not merely to speed up existing processes, it is to enable entirely new ways of organising work. That was precisely the shift we had started to see. The agent didn't just do the work faster; it changed the nature of the work altogether. Staff no longer needed to be deployed in firefighting mode to keep up with peak volumes. Instead, they could shift focus to strategic planning, student onboarding, or real-time enrolment data analysis, work that had a greater impact on outcomes and organisational improvement.

This aligns with Peter Drucker's (1966) vision of technology as a liberating force. He famously observed that the true promise of innovation lies in its ability to "free up human effort for more meaningful activity." That is exactly what happened. AI enabled us to refocus some staff attention from the transactional to the transformational. No longer weighed down by repetitive tasks, certain colleagues could now apply their skills to areas that required judgement, empathy, and insight, human capacities that no algorithm can replace.

Furthermore, this shift had implications for staff morale and well-being within the areas benefiting. Reducing repetitive, mentally fatiguing work allowing staff to engage in complex, purposeful tasks with clarity and focus.

Efficiency also became a strategic enabler. Freed-up capacity meant that those teams could pilot new projects, explore service enhancements, and contribute to continuous improvement without the sense of "always being on the back foot."

In short, efficiency was not an end in itself. It was a gateway to empowerment, the kind that enables staff to do their best work, for the greatest good, with a renewed sense of clarity, control, and contribution.

Enhancing Staff Capability and Confidence

One of the most affirming outcomes of our AI implementation was the improvements in staff confidence and digital capability. Despite initial concerns, understandable in the face of media narratives about automation and job displacement, our approach did not diminish the role of staff. For many, it strengthened it.

From the outset, we took the view that AI should augment, not replace. That meant embedding staff not just in the use of AI tools, but in their design and development. Through collaborative co-design sessions with stakeholders, sandbox testing, a rigorous red-teaming process, and freedom to experiment and innovate, staff moved from passive recipients of technology to active participants in shaping it.

This shift supports the idea that learners achieve the most progress when supported by structured guidance that bridges the gap between what they can do independently and what they can achieve with assistance. In our case, that "scaffolding" took multiple forms: training sessions tailored to job roles or applications, hands-on experimentation with emerging tools, and peer-to-peer support embedded in professional learning communities.

As staff experimented in a low-risk environment, where there was no expectation of perfection, they developed a deeper understanding of not just what AI could do, but how and when to use it responsibly. They became more fluent in the use of AI, prompt design, more critical in assessing AI-generated outputs, and more thoughtful in identifying where human expertise remained essential. What emerged was a new kind of digital fluency: not just knowing how to use the tool but knowing how to interrogate it.

As large pockets of staff engaged with AI in meaningful, context-driven ways, they experienced mastery experiences, successes that reinforced their competence and motivated further engagement. These experiences were powerful enablers of behavioural change. They made the abstract concrete and the intimidating manageable.

The effects rippled beyond the technical. Colleagues who once felt overwhelmed by rapid digital transformation began to see themselves as contributors to innovation, not casualties of it. They gained language, tools, and confidence to engage in conversations about AI with nuance and insight. This, in turn, supported a culture of collective efficacy, a group's shared belief in its capability to organise and execute the actions required to achieve shared goals.

Importantly, this was not just about upskilling. It was about restoring agency. In a sector where staff often feel overworked, undervalued, and disempowered by bureaucracy, our AI strategy created new space for creativity, leadership, and growth. It reminded us that digital transformation done well isn't about replacing people, it's about investing in them. And that investment was beginning to pay dividends not just in capability, but in culture.

As one staff member reflected during a red-teaming session:

> *"I was worried AI would make my job irrelevant. But now I feel like I'm ahead of the curve. I understand it. That's empowering." Member of Support Staff*

That sentiment encapsulates the core of what we achieved. We didn't just build digital tools. We built digitally confident professionals, and in doing so, ensured that AI became a partner in progress, not a threat to purpose.

Elevating the Student Experience

Perhaps the most deeply human outcome of our AI strategy was the innovation it brought to the student experience. At the heart of this shift was the previously explained Student Buddy. Far from being a gimmick or a superficial chatbot, Student Buddy became a trusted companion for the students using it, navigating the many small but significant complexities of college life.

Available 24/7 via desktop, mobile, or laptop, and authenticated through our secure sign on, Student Buddy allowed students to self-serve on a wide range of questions. It pulled live data from our MIS and other systems, but it responded in the student's preferred language, and was embedded with custom logic to reflect the nuances of college policies and support systems.

In doing so, it democratised access to information. Students no longer needed to wait for office hours, queue at the desk, or feel anxious about asking "silly questions." Student Buddy offered them an immediate, non-judgemental interface, a safe, private, and accessible tool that gave them ownership over their time and their well-being.

This directly aligns with Maslow's Hierarchy of Needs (1943). At its most basic level, Student Buddy addressed lower-tier needs such as safety and certainty: timely, accurate information about exams, attendance, timetables, and college processes. But as students grew more confident in using the tool, they began to access more sophisticated support, on mental health, and academic advice, moving them up the hierarchy towards a sense of belonging, esteem, and ultimately self-actualisation.

For some students, Student Buddy became another way to seek help. The privacy and responsiveness of the agent meant students could ask questions that perhaps they might not otherwise ask. Importantly, the agent wasn't designed to replace human contact, it was designed to amplify it. Where appropriate, it redirected students to pastoral teams, safeguarding officers, or academic tutors, ensuring that support was not just accessible, but intelligently triaged. Student Buddy acted as both a digital concierge and a personalised learning support tool, helping students make sense of the wider system while maintaining their autonomy within it.

Moreover, its accessibility features, including voice-to-text, screen reader compatibility, dark/light modes, and multilingual support, meant that we weren't building one tool for "most" students and another for those with additional needs. We were building one tool for everyone, with inclusion designed into the architecture.

The result was a shift in how some students accessed services and information. For those using it, they no longer saw support as something that lived behind a door or depended on staff availability. They began, albeit slowly at first, to see it as something embedded into the fabric of their daily college experience, intelligent, responsive, and always available.

As one student from my tutor group shared in a feedback session:

> "It's like the college is finally speaking my language... literally. Student Buddy knows what I need, when I need it. And when it can't help, it tells me where to go. It's like having the college in my pocket." Jenny (Second Year)

Thus, AI became more than an operational tool. It became a student success tool, one that can reduce friction, increase confidence, and help ensure no student falls through the cracks due to a missed message, a closed office, or a fear of asking for help.

A Culture of Continuous Improvement

Another significant advantage of developing our own AI tools was the level of agility and responsiveness we retained throughout the process. Unlike many educational institutions locked into commercial software platforms with fixed development cycles, we retained full control over the development pipeline. This meant that we could respond to live feedback from staff and students with real-time adjustments, without waiting for delayed product updates, or complex procurement routes.

This model mirrored the Deming Cycle, the well-established Plan-Do-Check-Act (PDCA) framework for continuous improvement (Deming, 1986). Each agent was conceptualised (Plan), built and tested (Do), evaluated through feedback and red-teaming (Check), and refined or re-deployed (Act). And then the cycle began again. This iterative, circular approach wasn't just a technical benefit; it was a cultural one. It reinforced the idea that AI was not a one-off project, but a living system, evolving as the needs of the college evolved.

For example, when staff encountered confusing outputs from an early version of the results agent, they were able to flag the issue, suggest a change, and see that change implemented within hours.

Prompts were re-engineered to improve clarity. Filters were added to reduce ambiguity. Safeguarding guardrails were strengthened in response to specific use cases raised by our red team. None of this required time-consuming escalation or a six-month wait for a version update. We were in control, working alongside our developer, and with that control came responsiveness and resilience.

This approach aligns with the principles of Agile development (Beck et al., 2001), which values individual interactions over processes, working tools over comprehensive documentation, and responding to change over following a plan. These principles became embedded in our operational rhythm. We didn't aim for perfect tools, we aimed for useful tools, made better with every iteration.

Crucially, this iterative culture fostered a deeper sense of shared ownership. AI wasn't something being imposed by a central team; it was something being shaped collaboratively by stakeholders across the organisation. As feedback loops tightened and changes became visible, the staff involved began to see themselves as co-creators of the tools they relied on.

This is an example of people continually expanding their capacity to create the results they truly desire, and where collective intelligence drives innovation. By making every agent an opportunity for feedback, learning, and refinement, we made improvement a shared habit.

Importantly, this agility ensured relevance. In a fast-moving field like AI, the shelf life of a good idea can be short. What worked last month may be outdated next term. By keeping development close to the front line, we could ensure that our tools kept pace not only with technological evolution, but with local context, policy changes, staffing shifts, and student needs.

In this way, our bespoke solution model didn't just help us move faster. It helped us learn faster, building confidence, capability, and commitment with every cycle.

Embedding Inclusion and Ethical Practice

From the outset, our AI development was anchored in ethics, not as an afterthought, but as a design principle. We recognised early that in the rush to adopt emerging technology, many organisations risk compromising their values in pursuit of functionality. We were determined to avoid that path. Instead, our commitment was aligned to Responsible Research and Innovation, as defined by Stilgoe, Owen, and Macnaghten (2013): a framework built on the pillars of anticipation, inclusion, reflexivity, and responsiveness.

This meant we didn't just ask, "Can this be done?" but always followed with, "Should it be done? For whom? Under what conditions? And with what safeguards?" Every AI agent we developed, whether internal-facing or student-facing, was scrutinised through an ethical lens. Each system had embedded guardrails: prompt constraints, content filters, audit trails, and red-teaming processes that deliberately tested for vulnerabilities in safeguarding, inclusivity, and potential for bias.

Our red teams were not simply testing functionality. They were stress-testing ethical resilience, trying to surface responses that could harm, mislead, or exclude. We actively encouraged testers to probe the agents with inappropriate, controversial, or ambiguous prompts, understanding that the cost of a weak response wasn't just reputational, but potentially pastoral or even legal.

A particularly powerful application of this ethical-by-design approach was in Student Buddy, our student-facing AI assistant. Recognising that students engage with technology in diverse ways, Student Buddy's accessibility functions were deliberate expressions of inclusion, signals to our students that AI would not exclude or flatten their identities but meet them where they were.

Moreover, the ethical stance extended to data handling and transparency. Every query and response was logged, not as surveillance, but to safeguard. This audit trail allowed us to track the use of agents for safeguarding concerns, respond to queries flagged as high risk, and continuously improve based on real-world usage patterns. By housing everything within our domain, we retained complete control over data flow, user authentication, and consent pathways, particularly important for under-18s.

We weren't just building efficient tools. We were building fair ones, tools that understood the plurality of human experience and sought to serve it with integrity. We resisted the urge to outsource the ethics to external platforms. Instead, we brought ethics in-house, embedding it in every decision, every line of code, and every user interaction.

The result was not perfection, but responsiveness. A system we could adjust, a culture we could grow, and a platform we could trust. We demonstrated that it's not only possible to innovate without compromising values, but it's also more sustainable, more inclusive, and ultimately more powerful to do so.

Strategic Alignment and Organisational Learning

While many of the early benefits of our adoption of AI were tactical and immediate, reducing workload, improving accuracy, and enhancing service access, the deeper value emerged in how AI began to shape elements of our strategic direction and organisational mindset. Rather than being an add-on or a side project, AI became a driver of institutional alignment, influencing how we defined success, prioritised resources, and sustained change.

We were intentional about ensuring that every AI initiative, every agent, every prompt, every integration, was mapped against the college's strategic objectives. Whether it was reducing administrative workload, supporting well-being, improving safeguarding compliance, or advancing our digital agenda, each agent was developed to serve a clearly defined organisational goal. This mirrors the Burke-Litwin Model of Organisational

Performance and Change (1992), which emphasises that sustainable transformation requires deep alignment between an organisation's systems, structures, and strategy.

In this model, change in one domain (such as technology) only becomes meaningful when it aligns with other key drivers, such as leadership behaviour, organisational culture, and external environment. Our agents didn't simply replace manual processes. They helped reshape workflows, supported decision-making, and surfaced new performance metrics. AI became part of the system, not a tool outside it.

As we developed and deployed each agent, we discovered that they were not only delivering technical value, but they were also generating learning. Every round of prompt engineering, every user feedback session, every red-team test unearthed insights not just about the technology, but about ourselves: how we work, how information flows (or doesn't), where policies are unclear, or where staff and students feel unsupported.

Each agent project became a microcosm of the learning cycle. We learned what data we lacked or had duplicated, what questions we weren't asking or had multiple answers to, and what friction points existed between teams, systems, and services.

For instance, in developing Certificate AI, we uncovered inefficiencies in how results data was prepared and validated. And in piloting Student Buddy, we learned more about student navigation patterns, pain points, and access barriers than any survey had ever revealed. These were unexpected, strategic insights, lessons that fed directly into policy reviews, training programmes, and system redesigns. AI helped us identify not just what wasn't working, but in many cases, why it wasn't working, prompting deeper reflection and more intentional innovation.

And perhaps most importantly, this learning was not isolated to the small project team. Because development and testing were co-created with groups of staff and students, the lessons became shared knowledge, referenced in cross-team conversations, and used to inform future innovation roadmaps. We developed new governance mechanisms (like our AI policy and guidance documents), updated organisational risk registers, and began planning with a sharper understanding of both technical opportunity and organisational readiness.

In this way, AI became a mirror and a compass, reflecting our current systems, while helping us navigate where to go next.

Conclusion: The Real Benefit? A Culture of Possibility

In the end, the real value of our AI journey lay not just in what we built, but in what we became. The agents we developed may have saved some hours, improved accuracy, and streamlined workflows, but the most profound shift was cultural. We stopped asking how AI could fit into education, and started asking how education could evolve because of AI.

We didn't just automate processes. We created space: for staff to think strategically, for students to access help on their own terms, and for the college to reflect, adapt, and grow. We weren't chasing innovation for its own sake. We were embedding it, carefully, ethically, and inclusively, into the lifeblood of our institution.

This evolution reflects what Michael Fullan (2001) describes as a "deep change" transformation that redefines relationships, refocuses values, and retools systems from the inside out. Our AI implementation didn't just improve performance; to an extent, it enhanced our collective capacity. It turned some technophobia into fluency, some disconnected services into coherent ecosystems, and digital uncertainty into strategic confidence.

Just as Everett Rogers' (2003) Diffusion of Innovations theory reminds us, the success of any innovation is contingent not only on the strength of the idea, but on the culture into which it is introduced. Our greatest achievement was having the kind of culture where AI could take root: one of trust, openness, continuous learning, and shared purpose.

AI didn't replace people, it empowered them. It didn't eliminate human touch, it helped to amplify it. And it didn't create a monolithic system, it inspired a dynamic, evolving framework where the college could think, learn, and act more intelligently at every level.

For us, we didn't just implement artificial intelligence. We began to cultivate institutional intelligence.

And so, as we look to the future, we do so not with a fixed roadmap, but with a mindset of curiosity, courage, and co-creation. The benefits of AI in education are real, but they are not automatic. They are unlocked through design, through dialogue, and through a deep commitment to purpose.

What we've learned is that digital transformation is not about replacing what works. It's about reimagining what's possible.

And that, perhaps, is the most important lesson of all.

Chapter 5: 📖 What We Learned

- AI can do more than save time, it can improve staff capability, confidence, and inclusion.
- Operational efficiency enables staff to reinvest energy in high-value, human-facing work.
- When thoughtfully deployed, AI reinforces organisational learning and strategic alignment.
- The real return is a culture of continuous improvement, not just productivity gains.

Chapter 5: 💡 Key Reflection Questions

- How is AI currently supporting, or how could it support, improvements in staff efficiency and well-being?
- In what ways are you using AI to enhance the student experience beyond the classroom?
- Are your AI tools contributing to a culture of continuous improvement across teams and departments?
- How are you measuring the impact of AI adoption on operational performance and capacity gains?
- What mechanisms are in place to ensure AI use aligns with your institution's core values and educational mission?
- How are you equipping staff with the skills and confidence to innovate with AI in their own roles?
- Are you intentionally designing for scalability and sustainability from the start?
- What success stories can you share internally to build momentum and belief in your AI strategy?

CHAPTER 6: LEADING A CULTURAL SHIFT

When we first began discussing the implementation of artificial intelligence, the conversation was rooted, quite sensibly, in the practicalities of systems, efficiency, and measurable impact. We had operational challenges to address. We were facing staffing pressures, increasingly complex compliance demands, and a growing need for agile, responsive systems that could help us do more with less. In short, we wanted to solve real problems: to save time, reduce errors, and improve access to information and support for both staff and students.

But as the journey progressed, it became increasingly clear that while the tools we were building were impactful, the most profound change wasn't technological, it was cultural. What began as a project about efficiency quickly evolved into a conversation about identity, agency, and values. AI was beginning to shift from being a thing we used to a catalyst for how we think, how we lead, and how we collaborate.

This chapter is about that transformation. It's about the subtle but significant shifts in mindset, language, relationships, and expectations that took place as AI moved from the periphery of our college operations more towards the centre of our shared professional lives. It's about how conversations started to change, how confidence began to grow, and how, for many, curiosity replaced fear. It's about leadership, not as a title, but as a practice of modelling, inviting, and enabling change.

More than anything, this chapter is about culture as capability. It's about how we started to move beyond implementation to ownership, beyond buying into a trend, to building a future. What follows is a reflection not on the technical deployment of AI, but on the human dynamics that made it possible: trust, inclusion, shared purpose, and a willingness to learn together.

Because ultimately, our AI journey wasn't just about building tools. It was about cultivating a community capable of shaping and sustaining its own future.

From Compliance to Curiosity

At the outset, many colleagues understandably approached AI with a sense of cautious compliance. They turned up to briefings, tested tools when prompted, and completed sandbox tasks with polite professionalism. But underneath that surface-level participation was a very real and relatable blend of uncertainty, apprehension, and quiet scepticism.

For some, AI felt abstract, technical, unfamiliar, and distant from the relational, human-centred nature of education. Others viewed it as a potential threat to their role or professional identity. Questions buzzed quietly beneath the surface: What exactly is this technology? Is it safe? Is it just another trend? Will I be expected to become an expert overnight?

We quickly realised that no amount of top-down implementation would shift these perspectives. As Fullan (2007) reminds us, "You can't mandate what matters." Real engagement with innovation can't be compelled through compliance; it must be cultivated through relevance and trust.

To move past uncertainty, we had to foster not just understanding, but curiosity. We knew this wasn't a training problem, it was a confidence and culture opportunity. So, rather than "rolling out" AI, we invited people into it. We created spaces where curiosity could take root, non-judgemental, informal environments that encouraged exploration over expertise.

We ran sessions where colleagues could play with prototype agents or other tools at their own pace. We hosted red-teaming sessions where they could stress-test agents and openly discuss vulnerabilities and edge cases.

This approach mirrored the principles of "social constructivist theory" (1978), which suggests that learning is most powerful when scaffolded within a community of practice, where knowledge is co-constructed, not passively received. We didn't treat staff as users, but as co-learners and co-creators, and that changed everything.

Over time, something shifted. The questions got better. Staff didn't just ask "Can it do this?", but "Should it do this?" They started to move beyond fear of the unknown to critical curiosity. Suggestions became more frequent and more specific. Colleagues began shaping prompts, developing tools, proposing new use cases, and spotting limitations we hadn't anticipated.

This shift, from passive compliance to active curiosity, was subtle, but profound. It was moving AI from being something done to people, to something done with them. It turned implementation into conversation. And it unlocked a deeper form of engagement: not just using AI, but interrogating and improving it.

Importantly, this wasn't about turning everyone into a technologist. It was about making room for people to feel safe enough to ask, supported enough to try, and confident enough to lead. We were creating mastery experiences, moments where staff succeeded in small ways, built self-efficacy, and saw that they could shape innovation, not just survive it.

By creating the conditions for curiosity over compliance, we laid the groundwork for a culture where the staff that participated didn't just accept change, they owned it.

Redefining Professional Identity

One of the most subtle, yet most powerful, shifts we observed throughout our AI journey was in how staff began to see themselves, not just in relation to the technology, but in relation to their evolving roles and value within the college. At the outset, it was perfectly natural for some to fear that AI might diminish their contribution. There were quiet concerns: Will this replace what I do? Will my knowledge still matter? Am I being automated out of relevance?

But what emerged was something far more hopeful and empowering: AI didn't erode professional identity, for many it evolved it.

Educators, for instance, who once feared that AI might undermine their expertise, began to reimagine their workflows. Rather than viewing AI as a competitor, they began to treat it as a collaborator, a tool that could streamline administrative duties, surface data-driven insights, or offer starting points for creative planning.

Administrative colleagues underwent a quiet transformation. Staff who had spent years navigating complex spreadsheets, email chains, and approval loops became, quite literally, prompt engineers. They learned how to structure instructions for AI agents, refine outputs, and integrate them into workflows. Their knowledge of "how the college works" became more important than ever. They weren't displaced, they were rediscovered as operational problem-solvers and digital translators.

Support teams, those on the frontline of well-being, safeguarding, and student services, found themselves stepping into roles that required them to interpret AI-generated information, flag concerns, and ensure that students remained central in a system increasingly mediated by technology. They became critical friends to the machines, ensuring that empathy, nuance, and equity remained at the heart of digital service design.

This transformation of identity wasn't superficial. As staff began to experience success using AI tools, successes that were concrete, contextual, and often surprising, they gained not only technical skill but also confidence and agency.

The professional growth that followed wasn't accidental, it was designed. We deliberately created opportunities for mastery experiences, collaborative problem-solving, and peer demonstrations and learning. Staff weren't told what to do with AI, they were asked what they were doing with it and given the opportunity to showcase it. That distinction gave them permission to lead, adapt, and experiment on their own terms.

Importantly, this was never about turning teachers into technicians or frontline staff into coders. Our goal was not technical transformation, but human amplification. We didn't want to replace professional judgement; we wanted to liberate it. To elevate creativity, empathy, and insight by reducing the burden of repetitive tasks, fractured systems, and digital bureaucracy.

In many ways, AI became a mirror, reflecting the often-invisible expertise that staff had been deploying all along. And in that reflection, they saw something new: not a threat to their value, but a platform for it.

This, perhaps more than any agent or algorithm, was the true shift. The emergence of a professional culture that no longer asks, "What will AI do to us?" But instead, "What can we do with it?"

Leadership as Culture-Making

Leadership during this phase of AI integration was not defined by grand strategy documents or top-down directives. It was something far more relational and dynamic. It was about creating the conditions in which change could take root and flourish, not through authority, but through authentic participation.

Our SLT modelled the engagement we wanted to see from any member of staff. They attended the same CPD sessions as staff, not as observers, but as learners. They joined red-teaming exercises, tested agents, and even more importantly, shared their ideas, and their vulnerabilities. We saw leaders asking, "Can someone explain this bit to me?" and "What would you do differently?" That mattered. It shifted the tone of the entire programme.

This style of leadership aligns with Edgar Schein's (2010) definition of organisational culture as "a pattern of shared basic assumptions that the group learns as it solves problems of external adaptation and internal integration." In other words, culture isn't declared, it's lived. It's shaped by what leaders consistently model, reward, and tolerate.

By showing that it was okay not to have all the answers, to experiment without fear, and to acknowledge missteps as part of the process, we as leaders created something incredibly rare and powerful: psychological safety. According to Amy Edmondson (1999), psychological safety is the belief that one can take interpersonal risks, ask questions, challenge ideas, admit mistakes, without fear of embarrassment or punishment. It's the soil in which innovation grows.

And for us, that soil was carefully nurtured. Staff began to take more risks with their ideas, not because they were told to, but because they knew they wouldn't be ridiculed or ignored. They saw the same behaviours mirrored at the highest levels of the organisation. This alignment between leadership practice and organisational values turned AI exploration into a shared cultural project, not just a departmental one.

Importantly, this was not a culture of reckless experimentation. It was a shift from being risk-averse to risk-aware. As Heifetz and Linsky's (2002) Adaptive Leadership model suggests, leaders facing complex change must distinguish between technical challenges (those with clear solutions) and adaptive challenges (those that require new learning, experimentation, and even shifts in values). Implementing AI in an education setting was firmly in the adaptive category. There was no playbook, just purpose, people, and the courage to proceed without guarantees.

By engaging visibly in this process, our leadership team did something more significant than deliver a programme. They dismantled the hierarchy of expertise. They made it clear that everyone, regardless of role or title, had something to contribute, and something to learn. That leadership wasn't about having the best answers, but about holding space for the best questions.

This inclusive, participatory style of leadership helped shape a culture where reflection was valued as much as action, where iteration was expected, and where ownership was distributed. It turned AI from a "project" into a small movement, because staff felt safe, seen, and supported.

That shift, from leadership as control to leadership as culture-making, wasn't just important. It was essential.

From Users to Co-Creators

One of the most important features of our AI journey was the principle of co-design. We made a conscious decision early on: this would not be a programme "done to" people, but "done with" them. Transparency during the process was non-negotiable. Every AI-powered tool or interaction was clearly labelled to ensure users knew they were engaging with artificial intelligence.

We didn't unveil polished, finalised AI agents planned behind closed doors and expect enthusiastic adoption. Instead, we invited staff and when appropriate students, into the development process from the very beginning. We brought rough ideas, wireframes, and imperfect prompts into agent development discussions, INSET day workshops and feedback loops, not to defend them, but to refine them together.

This approach was more than just a methodology. It was a move away from hierarchical assumptions about who holds expertise, towards a belief that those who use the systems every day, those closest to the work, are also closest to the best solutions. In doing so, we moved people from being users of technology to being shapers and co-authors of it.

This philosophy is deeply grounded in the co-creation model articulated by Sanders and Stappers (2008), which argues that innovation is most powerful when it emerges from the overlapping insights of diverse stakeholders, not from the isolated ideas of designers or executives. Co-creation isn't about consensus-building or mere consultation. It's about sharing power, inviting multiple perspectives into the creative process, and embracing complexity.

In practical terms, this meant that our AI development process was intentionally participatory. We ran sessions where teachers helped design prompts for feedback agents. Frontline staff collaborated on operational tools. Students tested early versions of Student Buddy, offering honest feedback about tone, accessibility, and relevance. These sessions didn't just improve the tools, they strengthened trust.

This approach flattened hierarchies. The most valuable insights often came from those with the most day-to-day contact with the problems we were trying to solve. Administrative assistants, safeguarding officers, IT technicians, students, all contributed meaningfully to the direction and creation of our AI infrastructure. In doing so, we surfaced challenges and opportunities that may never have been identified through a top-down approach.

Co-creation also embedded a deep sense of shared ownership. When people are involved in building something, they don't just understand it better, they care about it more. They advocate for it. They invest in its success. They feel empowered to critique it, improve it, and adapt it.

And this was not just inclusive, it was effective.

Agents designed through co-creation were more aligned to real needs, more sensitive to contextual nuance, and more readily adopted because they reflected the language, logic, and lived experience of their users. Technical design and cultural fit were not treated as separate workstreams, they were developed in tandem.

In fact, co-creation became an accelerant. It modelled the kind of values we wanted to scale; transparency, mutual respect, and iterative learning. Each co-design experience became a moment of professional development, not only enhancing digital literacy but building cross-functional relationships and strengthening organisational coherence.

Ultimately, by choosing to co-create rather than dictate, we signalled something powerful: we trusted our community to shape its own digital future. And in return, that community showed us what was possible when you make innovation a shared endeavour.

Embedding Language and Values

As our AI journey evolved, we realised that transformation didn't just require new tools, it required a new language. How we talked about AI shaped how people understood it. And how people understood it shaped how they engaged with it. This was about more than semantics. It was about culture. It was about values.

From the outset, we were intentional in avoiding the hype-laden, jargon-heavy terminology that too often surrounds emerging technologies. We knew that if we wanted AI to be inclusive and empowering, it had to feel accessible and grounded. So, we made a deliberate effort to develop a shared vocabulary, terms and concepts that demystified the tools and connected them to our mission.

We used phrases like bias, capability, agent, enhanced safeguards, agent confidence, do not answer accuracy levels, and context-aware prompting. These weren't technical terms for their own sake, they were cultural tools, enabling staff to have nuanced conversations about safety, ethics, and reliability without needing to be AI experts. Equally as important, we avoided referring to terms like "revolutionising", "transforming" or "leveraging". Terms that often carry more style than substance.

This language also helped us to reinforce and re-centre our core values, inclusion, safety, transparency, and empowerment. Every time we talked about AI, we linked it back to our strategic plan, our safeguarding responsibilities, and our commitment to student experience and success. We didn't treat AI as separate from our ethos, we embedded it within it. This echoed the principles of values-based leadership (Kouzes & Posner, 2002), where the most effective innovations are those that align closely with institutional purpose and moral conviction.

We also recognised that language is a lever of inclusion. For those who felt uncertain about technology, or who had been historically excluded from digital development work, being able to talk about AI in everyday terms was key. It made participation possible. It made experimentation safe. It ensured that AI wasn't the domain of the few, but the responsibility and opportunity of the many.

Perhaps more importantly, by carefully curating the language we used, we set the tone for how AI would be perceived, not as a threat or gimmick, but as a tool in the service of people. We avoided phrases like "automating roles" or "disrupting education". Instead, we spoke about creating capacity, supporting decision-making, and freeing time for what matters most. This shift in tone helped staff move from apprehension to engagement.

Language also played a central role in shaping expectations. We didn't promise perfection, we promised progress. We used phrases like prototype, beta version, red-teaming, and pilot. This framed each deployment not as a final product, but as a living, evolving system open to feedback. It reinforced that change was not being imposed, it was being invited.

And this mattered. Because in a period of significant transformation, where trust is fragile and uncertainty is high, the words we choose become the scaffolding of belief. Belief in the tools. Belief in the process. And belief in each other.

Ultimately, embedding language and values wasn't just about communication, it was about culture-building. It was about creating the linguistic infrastructure for a community to learn, adapt, and lead together. And it worked. By the time we were exploring our third wave of AI agents, most staff weren't just using the right vocabulary, they were asking better questions, surfacing deeper insights, and connecting AI to the very heart of our college operations.

That's the power of language. It doesn't just describe culture, it shapes it.

Making it Stick

If launching our AI tools was the first act, embedding them, truly making them stick, was the second. And this, as any leader of change knows, is often the more difficult phase. Because culture change is not an event. It's not a moment. It's a pattern, forged through consistency, reinforcement, and community investment.

We knew from the outset that enthusiasm alone would not sustain transformation. Without reinforcement, even the most exciting innovations risk becoming short-lived pilots, fondly remembered but quietly abandoned. So, we designed for longevity.

Staff and students were introduced to our AI agents not as novelties, but as part of the fabric of how we would like to work. They were shown how to use Bespoke LLM and Gemini, how to engineer prompts effectively, and how to escalate feedback or errors. From day one, the message was clear: these tools, although optional extras, were embedded, available, and designed to help.

For lots of staff, this message landed well. Many welcomed the clarity, the relevance, and the sense of capability it brought. But for students, the picture was more complicated.

While Student Buddy was positioned as a new standard in digital support, a trusted, 24/7 companion in navigating college life, it wasn't universally embraced. Despite its accessibility features, integration with the MIS, and sleek interface, student engagement posed challenges. And this wasn't due to poor design. It was cultural.

Young people don't typically do what adults tell them is "cool" or "innovative." In fact, the more we, as staff, celebrated or promoted Student Buddy, the more resistance we encountered from some students. If it was recommended in tutor sessions, plugged on the digital signage, and framed as the "next big thing," there was often a sense of eye-rolling detachment. As anyone who works in education knows, teenagers are incredibly adept at sniffing out adult enthusiasm, and instinctively rebelling against it.

Therein lay one of our most important lessons: true adoption isn't about endorsement, it's about relevance. For Student Buddy to work, it had to earn trust, not expect it. It had to meet real needs, in real time, in ways that felt authentic to students' lived experience, not just to the aspirations of the project team.

So, we adapted. We shifted from promoting features to letting students talk about it with their friends. Listening to their feedback and improvement requests. Slowly, organically, Student Buddy moved from being a staff-led tool to a student-used resource. Not because we pushed it, but because they pulled it, when it mattered to them.

We also embedded AI into our CPD programme, not as one-off sessions but as a continuous strand with an annual INSET day on AI for all staff. Training sessions weren't just technical, they were pedagogical, ethical, and strategic. Staff explored and demonstrated to colleagues how to adapt AI to their roles and how to use tools critically. We included space for uncertainty, for challenge, and for debate.

To maintain momentum, we established spaces for reflection and celebration. Some staff briefings became places to share AI success stories, not just the "big wins", but the small victories, a prompt or Gem that saved an hour. These stories weren't just updates. They were cultural messages, reinforcing what mattered.

We also democratised recognition. Colleagues who contributed to red-teaming or suggested prompt improvements were acknowledged. New use cases submitted by staff were explored, not dismissed. We created visible pathways for influence, ensuring that AI wasn't something done to people, but something shaped by them.

This echoes the principles of Kotter's (1996) eighth step of change: anchor new approaches in the culture. Tools were never just launched; they were integrated into shared purpose. We linked every agent back to strategic priorities, workload reduction, safeguarding enhancement, operational excellence, so that their relevance was reinforced not just in action, but in meaning.

And perhaps most importantly, we embraced imperfection as a norm. We didn't wait for tools to be flawless. We launched iteratively, updated frequently, and told people when something wasn't working. This transparency builds trust, and trust, as we've seen throughout this journey, is the bedrock of transformation.

In doing all this, we weren't just starting to embed tools. We were beginning to embed new habits, new expectations, and a new sense of what's possible. AI became less of a project and more of a practice. Less of a product, more of a partnership.

We had started to make it stick not because we mandated it, but because we modelled it, supported it, celebrated it, and, above all, shared it.

Conclusion: Culture as Capability

If this chapter has shown anything, it's that our greatest achievement wasn't the creation of AI tools, it was the cultivation of a culture capable of using them wisely. What started as a response to practical challenges, workload, efficiency, compliance, became something much more significant: a redefinition of how we think, work, and grow together as a college.

We didn't just adopt AI. We adopted a new mindset.

We moved from cautious compliance to collective curiosity. From fear of redundancy to a renewed sense of professional identity. From a top-down project to a shared, living practice. Along the way, we discovered that the true power of innovation isn't in the code, it's in the conversation. It's in the trust we build, the risks we share, and the willingness to learn, together, in the open.

This was never just a technological project. It was a human one. Because, as Edgar Schein reminds us, culture is not what we say, it's what we do, consistently, together. And in that doing, we redefined our norms. We created a culture where experimentation is safe, where feedback is invited, where every staff member feels like a co-author of the future, not just a recipient of change.

Importantly, we didn't achieve this through perfection. We achieved it through participation. Through red-teaming. Through co-design. Through asking hard questions and not pretending to have easy answers. Through celebrating the small wins and learning from the near-misses and failures. This wasn't smooth. But it was real.

And that reality is what will carry us forward.

Because AI will keep evolving. Models will get stronger. Interfaces will get slicker. New tools will emerge that render today's agents obsolete. That's inevitable. But the culture we've built, the language, the mindset, the shared values, that is what will endure.

Culture is not a by-product of innovation. It is its precondition.

And we now have a culture that is capable of doing more than reacting to change. We have one that is capable of leading it, with thoughtfulness, with courage, and with care.

In the chapters that follow, we'll move from culture to transformation, exploring how this shift is not just improving systems, but reshaping what it means to work, learn, and lead in a future-ready college.

Because the most important thing we built wasn't an AI agent. It was belief, in each other, in our shared mission, and in our collective capacity to shape what comes next.

Chapter 6: 🌍 What We Learned

- Lasting change comes from culture, not compliance.
- AI can reshape professional identity by elevating roles, not replacing them.
- Leaders must model openness, curiosity, and values-driven experimentation.
- Embedding shared language and clear values helps make innovation stick.

Chapter 6: 💡 Key Reflection Questions

- How are you fostering a culture of curiosity and openness towards AI across your institution?
- In what ways is AI adoption prompting a redefinition of professional identity for your staff?
- Are your leadership behaviours modelling the kind of risk-taking and experimentation you want to see?
- How are you enabling staff and students to move from passive users to active co-creators of AI tools?
- What language, stories, or metaphors are you using to embed your AI values into the culture?
- How are you reinforcing and sustaining cultural change beyond the initial excitement of new technology?
- Do your governance structures support inclusive decision-making and shared ownership of innovation?
- How are you recognising and celebrating those who contribute to the cultural shift?

CHAPTER 7: SCALING FOR THE FUTURE

By the time our AI programme had reached maturity in its first phase, we found ourselves standing at a new threshold. The tools had been built, tested, and started to become embedded. The cultural groundwork, so painstakingly laid through co-design, leadership modelling, and shared language, was now bearing fruit. Conversations about AI no longer started with "what is it?" but "what's next?" We were no longer pilots of innovation; we were practitioners of it. AI had moved from novelty to necessity. And so, the question became: what comes after the first success?

This chapter is about that inflection point. Not the beginning of innovation, but its continuation. Not about proving the concept, but about embedding it deep into the college operating system. It's about the second wave, the moment when ambition meets scalability, and when the decisions made can either entrench sustainability or stretch systems beyond their limit.

Scaling is not simply a matter of multiplying what works. It is an act of rebalancing, between freedom and consistency, experimentation and coordination, pace and patience. It requires us to think systemically: to ensure that as our tools expand in reach, they don't lose their relevance, and that as we invite more people into the work, we don't lose sight of the principles that made it work in the first place.

In this chapter, we explore what it meant to scale deliberately. To grow in a way that was agile but not hasty, confident but not careless. To ask not only "can we do more?" but "should we?" and "how will we know if it's working?"

This phase of our journey is far from complete but remains a work in progress. It will require a shift in mindset, from project thinking to platform thinking. From isolated use cases to interoperable systems. From champion-led success stories to institution-wide alignment. And it will likely require new infrastructure, governance models, resourcing strategies, and internal capability pathways that can sustain the work without stifling its creativity.

But at the centre of it all remains the same principle: AI should serve the college community, not the other way around. As the work expands, our values become even more important, not as slogans, but as signposts. This will keep us honest, keep us human, and ensure that scaling doesn't mean losing sight of what had made this work meaningful in the first place.

Scaling, in short, is not just a technical challenge. It is a leadership challenge. A cultural challenge. A test of our collective resolve to move from early adoption to enduring transformation.

This chapter unpacks how we might meet that challenge, what we might learn, how we might grow, and where we're going.

Building on a Strong, Localised Core

Unlike many organisations that rely on third-party AI platforms, our decision to develop our own solutions offered more than just a technical advantage, it provided architectural integrity. Every tool we built was not just technically embedded in our systems; it was culturally embedded in our institution. The prompts reflected our policies. The data sources were mapped onto our actual MIS structure. The workflows mirrored the reality of college life, from safeguarding escalation pathways to staff onboarding routines.

This wasn't a case of bending ourselves to fit the tool. The tool was built to fit us.

That distinction became increasingly important as we moved into a scaling phase. Because, unlike scaling a commercial SaaS solution, where growth often means more licenses, more cost, and more dependence, we were scaling a model of agency, not just technology. Every new agent we developed extended our own infrastructure, enriched our own ecosystem, and further consolidated our internal capacity. This was scalability by design, not by subscription.

Crucially, we weren't reliant on someone else's development roadmap. We weren't waiting for the next product release, update cycle, or customer support ticket to be resolved. When a new policy on student digital behaviour came into effect, we just had to submit a change request, and typically, the agent was updated that afternoon. When our staff suggested a change to improve output or enhance safeguarding, we were able to test it within days. When our MIS Manager spotted an inefficiency in results processing, we embedded a fix in the agent's logic within the hour.

This ability to respond immediately and precisely was not just efficient, it was empowering. It moved AI development from the periphery of organisational strategy to its core. It ensured that innovation was responsive to context, not abstracted from it. And most importantly, it enabled continuous alignment between our operational systems and our strategic ambitions.

Perhaps the most powerful outcome of this approach, however, is that scaling doesn't mean starting again. We don't need to re-pitch the idea, re-train the workforce, or reconfigure our processes. The foundations are already in place, technically, yes, but also psychologically and culturally. Staff aren't passive recipients of the next phase of work; they remain active contributors to it. Many have already participated in red-teaming, co-design, or prompt refinement. So, when we asked, "What should we build next?", the answers came from those who knew the problems best.

This is where our bespoke build model revealed its full strategic value. Scaling wasn't about expanding a product; it was about extending a capability. A capability that already lived within the agent, our people, our systems, and our culture.

In that sense, our infrastructure wasn't just robust, it was resilient. It could flex with our needs, grow with our ambition, and adapt without disruption. As Fullan (2006) argues, sustainability in education isn't about preserving what exists, it's about creating the conditions for continuous improvement. Our bespoke solution model didn't just support innovation. It institutionalised it.

And so, when the time came to scale, we didn't need to change direction. We simply needed to coordinate movement.

From Agents to Ecosystems

In the early stages of our AI journey, each tool was developed with a distinct and deliberate focus, solving specific problems with bespoke solutions. They were, by necessity, standalone agents: the Results Agent operated independently from Student Buddy, which had no connection to Certificate AI, and so on. But as adoption increased, and as staff and students began using these tools more frequently, the boundaries between them started to blur.

Use cases began to overlap, a safeguarding flag triggered by Student Buddy might be relevant to the information flowing through our Staff Assistant agent. Queries raised in our Bespoke LLM sometimes duplicated those answered by domain-specific tools. Prompt logic that worked well in one context could inform another. As usage grew, so did interdependence, and with it came complexity.

It became clear that we were no longer building isolated tools. We were building an AI ecosystem, a constellation of interconnected agents, data streams, and user interactions. This shift introduced a new set of design considerations: interoperability, data integrity, user authentication across agents, and the potential for unintended consequences if agents weren't synchronised effectively.

To manage this evolution, we recognised the need for structure without stifling, a governance model that would bring coherence, alignment, and ethical oversight without reverting to bureaucratic gatekeeping. Moving forward, the following formal AI governance framework, if implemented, would support both growth and integrity.

Key components:

- A rolling AI roadmap, integrated into the strategic planning cycle, ensuring that every agent under development was mapped to a long-term priority.
- An AI Steering Group, not dominated by technologists, but composed of representatives from all corners of the college: IT, curriculum leads, support services, safeguarding officers, and student voice. The diverse representation isn't tokenistic; it would ensure that decisions about deployment, ethics, and priorities reflected the full range of institutional perspectives.
- Standardised prompt and agent design templates, helping to reduce duplication, improve readability, and scale internal understanding. These templates would codify good practice, while remaining flexible enough to allow creative adaptation.
- Formalised feedback and evaluation loops, including usage analytics, staff and student surveys, and termly review panels. Each agent's performance could then be measured not only in time saved or queries answered, but in contribution to strategic objectives and lived user experience.

These systems would bring clarity, cohesion, and accountability to what could easily become a fragmented landscape of disconnected digital experiments. More importantly, they would enable us to treat AI as a system, not a set of siloed projects.

Rather than viewing AI implementation as a linear input-output pipeline, we must begin to treat it as a living network of feedback loops and shared dependencies. Every agent had upstream and downstream implications. Every prompt revision impacted not just one outcome, but potentially three others. Every user experience had the potential to influence trust in the wider AI infrastructure.

This shift also requires a change in language. We must talk less about "projects" and more about "capabilities." Less about "launches" and more about "versions." Less about "successes" and more about "systems resilience." The goal is no longer just to deploy functional tools, it is to build an infrastructure that can adapt, scale, and sustain innovation over time.

In doing so, we will also create space for more nuanced conversations about unintended consequences, overlapping access rights, bias reinforcement across agents, and the implications of composite data aggregation. These aren't just technical concerns, they are ethical, operational, and pedagogical.

Ultimately, governance isn't about controlling AI. It's about enabling AI to serve our mission safely, sustainably, and with integrity. It is about recognising that as tools become more intelligent, the systems that support them need to become more intelligent too.

And just as our tools have grown in complexity, so too has our understanding of what it means to lead in a digital institution, not by managing outputs, but by orchestrating systems that can listen, learn, and evolve.

Scaling Without Losing Trust

Perhaps the greatest challenge of scaling AI isn't technical, it is cultural. As more tools come online and increasing numbers of workflows become AI-augmented, we find ourselves grappling with a delicate paradox: the very success of our AI programme, its integration, ubiquity, and speed, poses a new kind of risk. The trust we had earned through transparency, co-design, and ethics-by-default is not a permanent achievement. It is a renewable resource, one that needs continuous reinforcement to remain credible.

The danger isn't resistance, it is complacency. As AI becomes more embedded in day-to-day operations, the novelty will wear off, but so too will the scrutiny. What had once been a cautiously co-created process risks becoming "just the way things are done." And with that familiarity comes a heightened responsibility to ensure that expansion didn't outpace reflection.

So, we have deliberately slowed down to scale up. We must reaffirm the commitments that have earned trust in the first place, not as static policies, but as ongoing practices woven into every stage of design, deployment, and governance.

- Every new agent will still be red-teamed, not by a small, isolated panel, but through wide participation. Staff from multiple departments and students from diverse backgrounds will be tasked with "breaking" the tools. They will be encouraged to stress-test for bias, misinterpretation, or inappropriate responses. Their provocations won't be treated as edge cases, they will be treated as early warnings.
- All interactions will be logged, reviewed, and auditable, not for surveillance, but for safeguarding, learning, and accountability. This living audit trail should become a cornerstone of our internal monitoring, allowing us to trace anomalies, examine usage trends, and intervene early when needed. In an environment of increasing automation, transparency becomes non-negotiable.
- The "100 per cent accuracy or do not answer" rule remains in place for all high-stakes functions, particularly those touching on safeguarding, medical advice, or personal academic data. In doing so, we send a clear message: speed and utility will never trump safety. As the

tools grow in sophistication, our threshold for reliability grows with them.
- We continue to use opt-in models and consent-based gating, especially for students under 18. Access to new agents will be scaffolded with clear information about functionality, data use, and limitations. Consent isn't a one-time tick-box exercise, it is a living conversation, embedded in onboarding, reinforced through tutorials, and revisited through feedback.

This isn't just a checklist. It is a cultural posture, one built on what Stilgoe, Owen, and Macnaghten (2013) describe in their framework for Responsible Research and Innovation (RRI): anticipatory, inclusive, reflexive, and responsive.

- Anticipatory, because we designed every agent with the assumption that its misuse was not only possible but probable without guardrails.
- Inclusive, because we deliberately brought in diverse voices at every stage, not just to validate ideas, but to challenge them.
- Reflexive, because we questioned not only what the technology could do, but what it should do, and what values it was embedding, reinforcing, or overlooking.
- Responsive, because when issues emerged, technical, ethical, or emotional, we were prepared to pause, adapt, and even withdraw agents where appropriate.

Scaling AI without scaling responsibility would be a short-lived victory. So instead, we will treat ethical oversight as a scaling function, not a cap on innovation, but its condition for legitimacy. Just as our systems grow more complex, our mechanisms for dialogue, governance, and reflection grow more mature.

This approach will remind us of a core truth often lost in the excitement of scale: the faster you go, the more deliberate you need to be. Cultural credibility cannot be retrofitted. It must be built alongside the system it is meant to uphold.

And in this way, what began as a question of infrastructure becomes something more enduring, a model of what it looks like to grow with integrity.

As we consider the future of AI within and beyond our college, it is vital to hold both optimism and caution in balance. The Agent Guide (2025) outlines two divergent futures for agent-based AI systems: an "Agent-Driven Renaissance" where AI supports well-being and expands opportunity, and an "Agents Run Amok" scenario, in which opaque, unregulated systems overwhelm human control and public trust. Our leadership decisions today will shape which of these futures becomes more likely. Scaling must therefore be grounded not only in operational confidence but also in ethical foresight. We must remain committed to transparent processes, inclusive access, and mechanisms that ensure we retain meaningful human oversight, even as AI becomes more autonomous and powerful.

Capacity as a Strategic Asset

As our AI ecosystem matured, it became clear that successful scaling wasn't just about increasing the number of tools, it was about increasing the number of people who could confidently use, support, and shape them. Technology alone cannot deliver transformation; it must be accompanied by a parallel investment in people and infrastructure.

We recognised early that the more our agents were embedded into daily workflows, the more staff and students would require timely, relevant, and accessible support. And not just in the immediate post-launch period, but continuously, as the tools evolved and as new users entered the system. So, we will take a proactive, systems-level approach to capacity building, expanding our internal knowledge base while reducing dependence on any one team or individual.

- We should establish AI Champions across departments, staff members nominated or volunteering to take on specialist roles in leading local adoption. These aren't just technical leads; they are contextual translators, responsible for helping colleagues apply AI within their specific operational or pedagogical setting. They should receive enhanced training, access to behind-the-scenes development updates, and structured time to coach others. Crucially, they would be embedded within teams, not apart from them, ensuring that support is both relational and relevant.
- We must formalise AI into our continuing professional development (CPD) provision, treating it not as a one-off trend but as a long-term learning strand. Alongside our annual Staff AI INSET Day, a celebratory showcase of projects, tools, and provocations, we can introduce micro-learning modules, short, role-specific tutorials and challenges that staff could complete throughout the year. These should be designed to build confidence incrementally, scaffolded by peer feedback, and accessible asynchronously to suit diverse working patterns.
- We can launch a Student Digital Leaders programme, not as a bolt-on enrichment offer, but as a key pillar of our scaling strategy. These students could be trained to support their peers in using Student Buddy and other agents, but more importantly, they could be invited into the design process itself. They can provide critical feedback, test language tone, question ethical implications, and help us identify blind spots, particularly around accessibility and user experience. Their insights will be fresh, honest, and often surprising, helping to ensure that our tools remain grounded in real student needs, not assumptions.

This model of distributed leadership closely mirrors Michael Fullan's (2007) concept of capacity building in educational change. Fullan argues that sustainable innovation doesn't come from top-down mandates or isolated training events. It comes from a culture of shared responsibility, where everyone is seen as both a learner and a leader. It depends on collective efficacy, the shared belief that the group has the capability to improve, and it is driven by learning-by-doing, not just theory or policy.

By adopting this model, we would be able to avoid common scaling bottlenecks. We won't centralise expertise, we multiply it. We won't treat digital confidence as an innate trait, we will nurture it. And we won't assume one-size-fits-all training would suffice, we will diversify our approach, recognising that confidence with digital/AI literacy, like confidence in any other domain, grows through relevance, practice, and supportive relationships.

Perhaps most significantly, this approach will embed the idea that innovation isn't owned by a tech team or led by a single leader. It is co-owned, co-led, and co-sustained by a distributed network of champions, coaches, and critical friends. In doing so, we won't just support scaling, we will make it resilient.

This distributed model creates a virtuous cycle. As knowledge spreads, confidence grows. As confidence grows, experimentation flourishes. As experimentation flourishes, impact deepens. And as impact deepens, more people will want to be part of the story.

Scaling, then, isn't just about growing the what. It was about multiplying the who.

Scaling Through Partnerships

As our AI maturity reached a new threshold, external interest followed quickly. Invitations arrived to speak at sector conferences, contribute to national working groups, and showcase our work across the UK's education network. Recognition was gratifying, but more than that, it was a call to service. We understood that leading in this space came with a responsibility to scale not just for ourselves, but with others.

So, we shifted our posture from institutional innovation to sector collaboration.

This meant making parts of our work explicitly shareable. Not polished "marketing" showcases, but usable resources grounded in day-to-day practice. We began documenting our work, not just what we did, but how we did it, and why. Our red-teaming approach, enhanced safeguarding practices for student-facing agents, and details of our AI ecosystem were collated, annotated, and released for others to explore.

Rather than protecting our intellectual property, we took inspiration from Henry Chesbrough's (2003) theory of Open Innovation, which proposes that organisations should benefit not only from internal ideas but also from engaging with external knowledge flows. In our context, that meant opening our doors, not closing them. Sharing what we'd learned, failures included, not to claim expertise, but to invite dialogue and co-creation. This led to the development of cross-institutional partnerships, where colleges and school trusts began collaborating to refine shared practices, approaches and tools.

We also contributed to policy conversations, sharing insights with the Department for Education, awarding bodies, other government departments, and regulatory agencies. Our emphasis on in-house development, ethical constraints, and co-designed adoption provided a counter-narrative to the often vendor-led AI discourse. We weren't advocating for one product or solution, we were advocating for a model of inclusive, anticipatory, and values-driven AI development within education.

And importantly, we didn't just speak at events, we helped curate them. By partnering with edtech organisations and academic institutions, we attended roundtables, published case studies, and supported the development of toolkits aimed at demystifying AI for education leaders. This positioned us not as an outlier, but as a contributor to a growing community of practice, a movement rooted in curiosity, caution, and collective progress.

The benefits of this approach were twofold.

First, it kept us sharp. By inviting scrutiny, feedback, and cross-sector collaboration, we were continually challenged to refine our thinking. We had to articulate our rationale, test our assumptions, and defend our design choices, not in isolation, but in community. That made us better.

Second, it reinforced our belief that responsible innovation is not a competitive advantage, but a shared obligation. In a sector as interdependent as education, where trust, safeguarding, and equity are paramount, it was clear that no single institution could "own" AI. What we could do was contribute. Offer. Iterate. And in doing so, help ensure that the future of AI in education is not dictated by commercial scale, but shaped by collective intent.

In many ways, this outward turn marked the final phase of scaling: not just expanding our reach, but deepening our role as stewards of a larger conversation. It was no longer about what we as an organisation could do with AI. It was about what we, as a sector, could imagine, build, and protect together.

And that spirit of openness, generosity, and shared responsibility will continue to guide us in whatever comes next.

The Future: Scaling with Purpose

Looking to the future, our ambition remains not to chase technological novelty, but to pursue meaningful progress. Scaling, for us, no longer means more agents, faster outputs, or broader automation for its own sake. It means asking better questions, deeper questions. The kind that interrogates not just what AI can do, but what it ought to do in the unique and human-centred environment of education.

This requires a shift in perspective: from solution-building to purpose-seeking.

We are now asking questions that stretch beyond efficiency and into equity:

- Where can AI be a lever to reduce disadvantage, not just workload?
- How might we deploy agents that meaningfully support SEND learners, not by simplifying content, but by tailoring delivery to individual cognitive, sensory, and emotional needs?
- Can AI help us see what we might otherwise miss, early signs of disengagement, drops in motivation, or subtle well-being patterns emerging across a cohort?

These questions are more than hypothetical, they're directional. They signal where our next wave of innovation must point: not towards convenience, but towards compassion. Not simply streamlining what already exists but transforming what could.

This reflects the shift from technical adoption to what Michael Fullan (2007) describes as the moral purpose in change leadership. It's the idea that system improvement is only meaningful when it serves learners more justly, more equitably, and more holistically. Technology, in this frame, is not the driver, it's the instrument of that purpose.

We are also beginning to explore AI's potential to enhance student voice at scale. Not through surveys or focus groups, but through pattern detection in anonymised queries, prompt analytics, and sentiment mapping. Could agents become early indicators of unmet needs, emerging anxieties, or hidden opportunities for support? Could they give leaders a deeper understanding of what students care about, struggle with, or aspire to, in real time?

Done well, this isn't surveillance, it's listening. It's building tools that can notice more, interpret wisely, and respond kindly. But doing it right requires rigorous safeguards, clear ethical constraints, and the continued application of what Stilgoe et al. (2013) describe as anticipatory governance, the practice of looking ahead to identify not just what might go wrong, but what might be done better.

That's why our ethical frameworks are not static. As capabilities expand, so must our capacity for reflexivity. With each new integration, whether AI-powered analytics, adaptive learning pathways, or triaged safeguarding alerts, we return to the questions that shaped our first agents:

- Is this equitable?
- Is this transparent?
- Is this empowering?
- Is this safe?

Because at scale, the stakes are higher. Small flaws amplify. Good intent isn't enough. Every AI interaction is also a human one, and so every decision we make must uphold the trust we've worked so hard to build.

To that end, we are adopting a multi-disciplinary lens on future development. Our upcoming explorations involve:

- AI-enhanced dashboards that help pastoral leaders see student risk more holistically.
- Agent-supported marking tools to reduce staff workload, improve consistency and ultimately improve student experience.
- A specific SEND tool to support the heavy administrative burden around access arrangements, EHCPs and annual reviews.

But each of these is being developed slowly, carefully, and in conversation with the communities they're meant to serve. This is not acceleration for its own sake. This is strategic patience, rooted in our founding principle: AI must serve people, not replace them, not surveil them, and never bypass them.

As we stand on this next horizon, our compass remains the same.

We're not just scaling tools. We're scaling judgement, humility, and care.

We're building not just an AI infrastructure, but an educational ecosystem that's more responsive, more inclusive, and more human because of it. One that recognises that true progress is measured not in hours saved, but in lives improved.

And that's a future worth scaling for.

Conclusion: Scaling as a Way of Thinking

Scaling, we've learned, isn't about making more. It's about making meaning. It's not a linear act of expansion, but a deliberate practice of refinement, of embedding, aligning, and evolving. For us, scaling wasn't just a technical feat; it was a cultural commitment.

We moved from individual agents to an ecosystem. From pilot projects to embedded infrastructure. From curiosity to coherence. At each step, we didn't ask; "What's possible with AI?" we asked; "What matters most now?" And we kept asking.

What made scaling sustainable wasn't velocity. It was values. We scaled trust by strengthening governance. We scaled capability by investing in people. We scaled relevance by listening, really listening... to what staff and students needed, even when it challenged our assumptions.

The result is not a finished system, but a living one. A college where AI is not a product to be deployed but a dialogue to be continued. Where every new agent is a conversation about ethics, every data points to an opportunity for inclusion, and every interaction a chance to build something better.

This is what it means to scale with integrity. To recognise that progress doesn't mean letting go of what we care about but doubling down on it. To understand that systems don't scale culture, culture scales systems. And to accept that the real measure of impact isn't how many agents we've built, but how deeply they've helped us stay human, responsive, and ready.

We're not finished. We're just beginning. Because scaling, at its best, is not a milestone. It's a mindset.

Chapter 7: 🧠 What We Learned

- Scale requires systems thinking, not just technical replication.
- Capacity, both digital and human, is a strategic asset for long-term transformation.
- Maintaining trust, purpose, and localisation is key when expanding reach.
- Partnerships and ecosystems will define the future of educational AI, not standalone tools.

Chapter 7: 💡 Key Reflection Questions

- How are you ensuring that your AI strategy can scale without compromising trust or quality?
- Are you building on a strong, localised foundation before expanding your AI capabilities further?
- What systems are in place to support interoperability, sustainability, and growth of your AI ecosystem?
- How are you using partnerships to accelerate innovation without losing institutional identity or control?
- In what ways are you treating staff time and capacity as strategic assets when planning to scale?
- What indicators or metrics are you using to know when to scale, and when to pause?
- How are you protecting the core values and cultural foundations that made your early adoption successful?
- Is your thinking around AI scaling as a technology, or as a mindset and leadership approach?

CHAPTER 8: LESSONS LEARNED AND GUIDANCE FOR EDUCATION LEADERS

The AI journey that we took was not just an exercise in technological transformation. It was a multi-layered organisational shift, strategic, cultural, and operational. From redefining workflows and automating labour-intensive processes, to cultivating trust, digital literacy, and shared ownership among staff and students, this journey touched every layer of college life. It reimagined not just what was possible with AI, but how we lead, collaborate, and make decisions in a digital-first world.

Chapters 1 to 7 have mapped that journey in depth, from building the first bespoke agents, to embedding AI in daily practice, to scaling responsibly and sharing learning with the wider sector. But implementation is only part of the story. For education leaders across the UK and beyond, the more pressing question is: What does this mean for us? What do we do next?

This chapter serves as a response to those questions. It is not a one-size-fits-all solution. Education is deeply contextual, and no two institutions are the same in their resourcing, governance, staffing models, digital maturity, or student demographics. There is no universal template that can be lifted and applied wholesale. What worked for us, worked because it was grounded in *our* values, *our* systems, and *our* people.

And yet, amidst that variability, there are patterns, principles that hold true across settings. The insights captured here are not prescriptive, but illustrative. They form a kind of blueprint, not for replicating our model, but for enabling leaders to shape their own. They are practical, but also philosophical. Because adopting AI is not just a technical decision; it is a leadership one. A cultural one. A moral one.

To adopt AI meaningfully and sustainably in your own institution means asking big questions:

- What kind of organisation do we want to be?
- What do we value about human expertise?
- Where are the barriers to success for our staff and students?
- And how might responsible AI help us reduce them?

These are not questions that sit with your IT team. They are questions for your senior leaders, your middle managers, your curriculum leads, and your pastoral teams. They are questions that require conversation, consultation, and courage.

In what follows, we do not offer a roadmap, but a compass. A distillation of the most important lessons we've learned, and the frameworks that helped us navigate uncertainty. Whether you're just starting out or already experimenting with AI in your institution, our hope is that these lessons serve as a guide, a way to move forward with clarity, integrity, and purpose.

Because ultimately, AI is not the change. *You* are.

The technology is a catalyst. The leadership is what makes it stick.

Establish an AI Policy, No Matter Where You Stand

First things first, whether your institution is all-in on artificial intelligence, cautiously curious, or still deeply sceptical, one thing is universally true: you need an AI policy.

Not a vague set of intentions. Not a hastily written FAQ. A real, tangible, institution-wide document that defines the boundaries, responsibilities, and expectations surrounding the use of AI by staff, students, and third parties. Without it, you are not leading AI, you are reacting to it.

We often hear education leaders say, "We're not ready for an AI policy, we haven't even started using AI yet." But this is precisely why you need one. If you don't set the rules of engagement, others will fill the gap. Students will bring generative tools into their coursework. Staff will quietly experiment with ChatGPT for lesson planning or reports. AI will find its way into your ecosystem whether you endorse it or not. The question isn't if, it's how, where, and with what oversight.

A robust AI policy isn't about endorsing or rejecting the technology. It's about creating clarity.

Clarity about expectations. What are staff and students allowed to do with AI tools? Can AI be used for assignments? For marking? For communication with parents? Without clear guidance, people will either take risks blindly or avoid innovation altogether for fear of misstep.

Clarity about accountability. If something goes wrong, an error in output, a misuse of data, a safeguarding concern, who is responsible? Who investigates? What thresholds are in place to escalate concerns?

Clarity about boundaries. What types of tools are acceptable? What data can be used to train models? Can generative AI be used for pastoral work? Can students opt out? These are decisions that must be made before the pressure to adopt becomes urgent.

Clarity about values. A policy doesn't just dictate what you can do, it declares what you stand for. A well-crafted AI policy is an extension of your institution's ethical code. It should reflect your commitment to inclusion, safety, academic integrity, and learner agency. And it should be developed collaboratively, with input from staff, students, governors, and technical specialists.

Critically, this policy should be living, not static. It must evolve with the tools, with the law, and with your internal understanding. But you can't iterate what doesn't exist. Starting now gives you a platform from which to lead responsibly.

Tip: Create your AI policy before you're "ready." Use it to open up discussion, not shut it down. Share early drafts with students and staff. Host workshops. Use it as a springboard for dialogue, development, and co-ownership.

You don't need to have all the answers, but you do need a framework for asking the right questions.

Because in the absence of a policy, people default to uncertainty. And uncertainty leads to risk, fear, or uncoordinated action. A good AI policy doesn't suppress innovation, it enables it, by giving your community the confidence to explore, experiment, and innovate safely.

Just as no school would function without a safeguarding policy, a behaviour code, or a data protection protocol, no institution in this new era should operate without clear guidance on AI.

Whether your stance is cautious, curious, or committed, write it down. Make it known.

Because leadership starts with clarity. And clarity starts with policy.

Lead with Strategy, Not Hype

Before the first line of code was written, we began with questions, not solutions. This was not accidental, it was essential. In a landscape saturated with hype, pressure, and vendor-driven narratives, the most powerful stance a leader can take is to pause and ask: *What are we actually trying to solve?*

Education leaders must resist the urge to adopt AI simply because it's trending, or because a neighbouring institution is piloting something new. AI is not a marketing badge or a technological trophy, it's a tool. And like any tool, its value depends entirely on the clarity of the problem it's designed to address.

For us, this began with honest reflection on our operational and strategic realities. Where were we losing time? Where were staff overloaded with repetitive, error-prone processes? Where were students experiencing friction or delay in accessing the support they needed? Just as importantly, what were our long-term goals, around inclusion, efficiency, well-being, and student experience? AI wasn't the answer until we were clear on the questions.

For leaders embarking on this journey, this is where you start, not with technology, but with *strategic alignment*. Ask yourself:

- What inefficiencies are eating into staff time or student learning?
- What compliance risks or administrative burdens are pulling focus away from core priorities?
- Where are students slipping through the cracks, academically, pastorally, or socially?
- What institutional goals are consistently under pressure, despite your best efforts?

From there, consider how AI might support, not supplant, your strategy. Could it reduce workload, increase consistency, surface hidden patterns, or extend access? If so, great. If not, wait.

Too often, AI projects fail not because the technology doesn't work, but because the rationale behind them was never clear. Adopting AI without a strategic purpose is like building a bridge without knowing where you want it to go. It looks impressive but leads nowhere.

Tip: Align AI initiatives with your existing strategic plan. If the problem it solves isn't already a priority for your senior leadership team, it probably isn't the right place to start. Your first project doesn't need to be flashy; it needs to be *felt*. A pain point that your community already understands, and will notice when it gets better.

The result? Early wins that matter. Credibility that builds. And a foundation for scaling AI that is grounded not in trend, but in transformation.

Start Small, Think Big

You don't need to overhaul your systems overnight. In fact, trying to do so is a fast track to overwhelm, disillusionment, and poorly integrated solutions. One of the key lessons from our AI journey is the power of starting small, *deliberately small*. Focus your early efforts on a specific domain where the problem is clearly understood, the process is repetitive and rule-based, and the potential for improvement is obvious.

Operational areas, such as enrolment, certificates, ID checking, or student communications, are ideal places to begin. These are typically low-risk, high-volume tasks where inefficiencies are well-documented, and the emotional stakes are lower than in teaching and learning. Automating or enhancing these workflows provides a clear, measurable return on investment, and allows the organisation to test both the technology and its own readiness for change.

We began with agents like the GCSE Results and Certificate AI. They didn't radically redefine what the college was, but they immediately improved how it functioned. One agent saving over 300 hours a year didn't just free up capacity, it shifted attitudes. It made AI *real*. Not abstract. Not future facing. But here, now, useful.

Once that first win is in place, momentum builds. Staff begin to see what's possible. Scepticism gives way to curiosity.

Conversations move from "Should we do this?" to "What could it do next?"

This approach mirrors principles from *Lean* and *Agile* methodologies, where early prototypes, Minimum Viable Products (MVPs), are used to generate learning, refine assumptions, and build internal confidence before scaling. It also reflects Fullan's (2007) guidance on sustainable educational change: start where change is achievable, demonstrate impact quickly, and then build outward.

Tip: Use early wins to secure long-term buy-in. A single AI agent that demonstrably saves 90 hours during enrolment, or eliminates a known bottleneck, can do more to shift mindsets than any slide deck or policy paper. Capture the data. Tell the story. Share the success. And use that credibility as fuel for what comes next.

Scaling AI isn't about doing everything at once, it's about *doing something that works*, and then using that success to unlock the next opportunity. Start focused. Stay flexible. Let momentum grow organically from real impact, not imposed timelines.

Own the Build Where You Can

Our decision to develop our own AI agents was not just a technical preference, it was a strategic imperative. By choosing to build within our own digital tenancy and using infrastructure we controlled, we were able to embed AI tools into the very fabric of how the college operates. This approach offered more than just convenience. It provided *architectural integrity*, data security, cost efficiency, and the flexibility to adapt at speed.

When agents like Student Buddy or the Certificate AI needed updates, whether due to a policy change, safeguarding requirement, or staff feedback, we weren't dependent on a vendor's release cycle or stuck behind a support ticket queue. In many cases we could respond in hours, not months. That kind of agility is almost impossible when relying entirely on commercial platforms.

More importantly, by retaining control over data flow, prompt design, and agent behaviour, we were able to embed our institutional values into the tools themselves. Safeguarding rules, consent protocols, ethical boundaries, accessibility features, these weren't bolted on. They were designed in from day one. This level of alignment is difficult to achieve through third-party solutions, especially when those platforms are designed for mass-market scalability, not sector-specific nuance.

That said, we recognise that not every college, trust, or school will have the in-house development capacity or financial resources to outsource production at the outset. But the lesson isn't "build everything yourself or don't bother." It's this: **move in the direction of internal capability over time.** Start with trusted partners or open-source frameworks if needed, but don't outsource your thinking, or your values.

Relying entirely on third-party tools brings significant risks:

- **Data governance and GDPR**: Who owns the data? Where is it stored? Is it being used to train commercial models?
- **Customisation limits**: Can you enforce your safeguarding requirements? Can you restrict outputs based on age, consent, or topic?
- **Cost escalation**: Subscription-based tools often scale poorly, what seems affordable now can become untenable at scale.
- **Exit barriers**: How easy is it to stop using the tool? Will your workflows break if the provider changes direction or pricing?

Tip: If you rely on external tools, do so with open eyes. Read the vendor's small print. Ask difficult questions about data handling, explain ability, model behaviour, and support commitments. And, crucially, build a roadmap to increase your internal capability over time. That might mean appointing an internal AI lead, investing in staff upskilling, or partnering with institutions that have already built their own tools.

Hybrid models can also be effective. For example, using commercial LLMs but deploying them through your own front-end interface, with your own prompts, filters, and logging mechanisms. The goal is to retain *agency*, even if you don't yet have full autonomy.

Because in the world of AI, control isn't about owning the most code. It's about owning the most *clarity*, over how tools are built, how they behave, and how they serve the people they're meant to support.

Focus on People, Not Just Products

Technology is inherently neutral, it doesn't arrive with values, priorities, or empathy. Its impact is shaped entirely by the context in which it's introduced. In education, that context is always human: it's shaped by relationships, trust, workload, and institutional identity. That's why simply *introducing* AI tools is never enough. Real adoption happens only when the culture around those tools invites exploration, builds confidence, and reinforces shared purpose.

We learned that staff will not adopt AI just because it's been made available. Nor will they engage meaningfully with it if they feel it's being imposed. What drives adoption is something far more organic: trust, in the tool, in the training, and in the people leading the change.

To foster that trust, we focused not on technology first, but on capability-building. We created a network of AI Champions across departments, colleagues with the desire, training, and encouragement to lead locally. They became the translators of innovation, able to connect college-wide strategy to everyday practice. Importantly, they were not expected to be technical experts. Their value came from understanding their domain, and being trusted by their peers.

We also invested in peer-led CPD. Rather than relying solely on top-down training, we built a model that allowed colleagues to share ideas, demonstrate agents in action, and problem-solve together. These sessions created safe spaces for experimentation, where staff could ask "silly questions" without judgement and feel reassured that uncertainty was normal. That sense of psychological safety was crucial.

Moreover, we acknowledged the range of digital confidence across our workforce. Not everyone needed, or wanted, to become an AI prompt engineer. Some simply needed to feel confident using a chatbot, adjusting a prompt, or recognising when a tool wasn't appropriate. So, we created tiered learning opportunities: micro-learning for beginners, sandbox play for intermediate users, and deep-dive sessions for advanced use cases.

Crucially, we gave people permission to play. We explicitly removed the expectation of mastery and encouraged experimentation. As Amy Edmondson (1999) argues in her research on *psychological safety*, innovation flourishes in cultures where people feel safe to fail. In our case, red-teaming workshops, feedback loops, and INSET days, helped turn tentative users into confident explorers.

The result? A shift from passive adoption to active engagement. Staff began contributing prompt ideas, spotting bugs, identifying use cases we hadn't considered, and even creating mini tools for their teams. They didn't just use AI, they *shaped* it. And in doing so, they changed the culture.

Tip: Build AI literacy before building AI systems. Your tools are only as effective as your people's confidence in using them. Literacy doesn't just mean knowing how to use a tool. It means knowing when to use it, when *not* to use it, and how to think critically about the results it produces. It means understanding the ethics, the boundaries, and the possibilities.

Because ultimately, culture eats strategy for breakfast, and *curiosity* will always be more powerful than compliance.

Design for Inclusion and Ethics from Day One

Safeguarding, privacy, and equity are not optional extras in AI implementation, they are foundations. Without them, the most advanced technology can quickly erode trust, amplify harm, or deepen existing inequalities. We discovered early on that responsible AI isn't just about what tools can do, it's about how those tools are governed, interpreted, and integrated into the life of an institution.

Our *"100 per cent accuracy or do not answer"* policy was a prime example. Technically, it meant that agents were instructed to remain silent when they couldn't generate a confident, accurate response. But symbolically, it communicated something much bigger: we valued truth and safety over speed or spectacle. It was a cultural signal to staff and students alike that we were not experimenting at their expense. We were building systems they could trust.

We also embedded logging and audit trails into every AI agent, not as surveillance, but as a safeguard. Every prompt and response could be reviewed. If something went wrong, or if something went unexpectedly right, we could trace it, learn from it, and adapt. These logs became not only a means of compliance (e.g., for GDPR and safeguarding standards), but also a tool for continuous learning and improvement.

The use of opt-in models, especially for under-18 students, reflected our commitment to consent-based innovation. Just because we had the technical ability to create agents for every function didn't mean we always should. We developed rigorous consent systems, linked to our MIS and agent access controls, to ensure students (and their parents or carers) had control over how and when they engaged with AI.

This level of care wasn't bureaucratic overhead, it was strategic infrastructure. It helped us move quickly without compromising principles. It also allowed us to build trust in stages, gradually extending functionality and user access in line with what we'd earned, not what we could engineer.

Equity, too, was central. We didn't assume every user had the same needs, digital literacy, or access. That's why Student Buddy was multilingual, voice-enabled, screen-reader compatible, and available on any device. And why every agent was reviewed for inclusivity in tone and output, as well as for technical performance.

But this isn't a static achievement. As AI tools evolve, becoming more predictive, more generative, and more embedded, the ethical questions will evolve too. That's why we advocate the creation of an Ethical AI Charter: a living document that defines your institution's values, boundaries, and non-negotiables when it comes to AI.

This charter should go beyond generic statements of principle. It should be specific, contextual, and actionable. For example:

- What types of decisions should AI *never* make?
- How will user data be handled, stored, and protected?
- Who will review and approve new AI tools – and how often?
- How will feedback, concern, or harm be escalated and resolved?

Tip: Create an ethical AI charter – and revisit it often. Use it as a guide for every development choice, from prompt engineering to deployment strategy. Involve staff, students, parents, and governors in shaping it. And as new capabilities emerge, let that charter evolve alongside them. Because ethical clarity today is the best defence against reputational and operational risk tomorrow.

In short, ethics isn't the *brake* on innovation, it's the *steering wheel*. It ensures you move fast and in the right direction.

In addition to designing for inclusion, education leaders must recognise that the next phase of AI integration will demand new forms of institutional responsibility. The field of agent governance offers a valuable framework to support this. For example, visibility interventions like agent IDs and activity logs help ensure AI systems remain accountable and traceable. Control mechanisms, such as shutdown protocols and restricted tool access, help institutions retain decision-making authority even in complex multi-agent environments. These tools, still in early development across the private and public sectors, can inspire educational leaders to adopt a governance mindset, treating AI not just as a technical system, but as a social infrastructure that must evolve with deliberate intent.

Think in Systems, Not Silos

As AI tools multiply, so too do their connections, to data systems, to workflows, to people. What begins as an exciting wave of experimentation can rapidly turn into an uncoordinated sprawl of tools and use cases, each evolving in different directions. Without clear oversight, this can lead to duplication of effort, inconsistent messaging, and even conflicts with institutional policy or safeguarding obligations.

That's why governance matters. We learned that AI innovation could only scale sustainably if it was supported by shared standards, transparent decision-making, and deliberate planning across functions. We didn't treat AI as a "bolt-on" to existing systems, we embedded it into the very architecture of how the college operated.

To do this, establish an AI Steering Group made up of staff from across the organisation: IT, operations, teaching, safeguarding, and student voice. This diverse membership isn't symbolic, it's essential. Each member brings a different lens to the conversation, ensuring that every new agent proposal is assessed not just for technical viability, but for cultural fit, policy alignment, and user impact.

We also introduced a rolling AI roadmap, aligned with the college's wider strategic goals. This wasn't just a project plan, it was a mechanism for *prioritisation*, ensuring that new tools were developed in a logical sequence and tied directly to known organisational challenges. By mapping AI initiatives to things that already mattered, like enrolment efficiency, safeguarding responsiveness, or digital inclusion, we avoided the trap of innovation for innovation's sake.

Equally important were our standardised design templates. Every agent followed a consistent structure: prompt libraries, guardrails, logging protocols, consent logic, and review mechanisms. This consistency reduced development time, made troubleshooting easier, and helped staff understand and engage with new tools more quickly. It also supported governance by providing a clear paper trail of who built what, when, and why.

This approach reflected key ideas from systems thinking (Senge, 1990), which encourages organisations to view change holistically, not as a set of isolated initiatives, but as part of an interconnected ecosystem. AI agents don't operate in a vacuum. They interact with MIS data, staff workflows, safeguarding frameworks, and learner expectations. As these dependencies multiply, so does the risk of unintended consequences.

Tip: Treat AI as part of your institutional architecture, not an add-on. That means:

- **Involving cross-functional voices** in every stage of development and decision-making.
- **Maintaining a live, accessible roadmap** of all AI projects in play.
- **Standardising agent design and deployment** with templates and shared protocols.
- **Reviewing agents regularly** for duplication, overlap, or conflict with evolving policies.

Ultimately, governance is not about slowing things down, it's about protecting your momentum. With clear structures in place, you can move faster, not slower, because you're building on stable foundations. You're not reinventing the wheel each time. You're scaling from a shared base of knowledge, values, and technical resilience.

In an AI-enabled future, your governance model will be just as important as your technical model. It's the difference between scaling chaos and scaling excellence.

Capacity Building Is Key to Sustainability

One of the most powerful enablers of sustainable AI transformation was our commitment to distributed leadership. Rather than centralising all knowledge, decision-making, and technical control within a single team or senior role, we deliberately invested in building capacity across the institution. This wasn't just a staffing strategy; it was a cultural choice.

AI Champions and Student Digital Leaders played a pivotal role in that strategy. These weren't token roles, they were agents of influence, embedded in every department and year group, acting as translators, trouble-shooters, and advocates. Because they were trusted members of their own communities, they had the credibility and local knowledge to bring others along on the journey, whether that meant answering a colleague's prompt-engineering question, collecting feedback on an agent, or co-developing new use cases.

This approach mirrors Fullan's (2007) theory of capacity building, which goes beyond technical skill development and focuses on fostering shared responsibility, leadership at all levels, and organisational learning. We weren't just training people to *use* AI; we were training them to *lead* with it. That's a critical distinction. AI became not just an operational toolkit, but a platform for distributed innovation.

It also reflected the principle of collective efficacy (Bandura, 1997): the shared belief that a group of people can successfully organise and execute the actions required to achieve desired outcomes. When staff and students saw their peers leading AI work, not just senior leaders or IT specialists, it created a sense of confidence and momentum. Innovation wasn't happening *to* them; it was happening *through* them.

This distributed model helped solve several common challenges in AI adoption:

- It prevented bottlenecks in IT or leadership teams, allowing faster response times for support, iteration, and experimentation.
- It normalised AI as part of everyday work, embedding it in the rhythm of departments rather than keeping it siloed in a tech programme.
- It supported a culture of feedback and iteration, with AI Champions feeding back on agent performance, user needs, and new ideas.

Just as importantly, it created space for differentiated learning. Not everyone engages with AI in the same way or at the same pace. Having Champions with varying levels of expertise and diverse job roles meant we could meet staff where they were, providing informal coaching, hands-on support, or peer-led training in ways that felt accessible and non-threatening.

Student Digital Leaders, too, were more than just helpers. They were co-creators, testing agents, suggesting features, raising ethical questions, and helping design communication strategies that resonated with their peers. Their insight ensured that our tools worked *for students*, not just in theory, but in practice. And in return, they gained authentic leadership experience, digital fluency, and a deeper understanding of the systems that shape their education.

Tip: Train for capacity, not just competence.

Don't just aim for a small team of AI experts. Build a broad coalition of confident, curious people across the organisation.

- Create visible roles for staff and students to lead, shape, and share AI work.
- Give them dedicated time (if possible) and development, not just extra tasks on top of busy workloads.
- Ensure their contributions are recognised, rewarded, and listened to.

The result? A college where AI wasn't a niche specialism or top-down mandate, but a shared language, spoken fluently by many, shaped collectively, and continuously evolving. When leadership is distributed, change becomes exponential. You don't scale tools, you scale people. And that's how real transformation happens.

Open Your Doors, And Your Thinking

True innovation doesn't happen in isolation. We quickly realised that the power of our AI journey didn't lie solely in what we built, it lay in how we shared it. From the outset, we adopted an "open innovation" mindset (Chesbrough, 2003), embracing the idea that institutional progress is amplified, not diminished, by transparency and collaboration.

This wasn't about charity or brand-building. It was a deliberate strategic choice. By engaging with other institutions, whether through presentations, resource sharing, or policy discussions, we created a feedback-rich ecosystem where ideas could be tested, refined, and scaled faster. When other colleges adapted our red-teaming protocols, prompt libraries, or ethical frameworks, they often improved them. And we listened, learning from their adaptations just as they learned from our origins.

In this way, sharing wasn't a loss of intellectual property, it was a multiplier. It turned isolated experimentation into sector-wide iteration.

This approach is grounded in what Wenger et al. (2002) define as "communities of practice" groups of people who share a concern, a set of problems, or a passion for a topic, and deepen their knowledge through regular interaction. AI in education is a perfect candidate for such communities. It is too complex, too fast-moving, and too ethically charged to be figured out alone.

By positioning ourselves as contributors rather than competitors, we expanded our own thinking. We learned how different contexts shaped implementation, where blind spots existed, and what barriers were common across institutions. This fed directly back into our internal development strategy, ensuring that our tools and principles were not just locally valid, but globally relevant within the sector.

It also supported what Hargreaves and Fullan (2012) call "professional capital", the shared wisdom, skill, and moral purpose that arises when practitioners collaborate deeply and regularly. Our AI agents became more effective because the people building them were in dialogue with others on the same path, asking better questions and surfacing new opportunities.

Critically, open innovation helped normalise responsible AI adoption across the further education sector. By showing what was possible, not through polished PR stories, but through real tools, live dashboards, and honest reflections, we gave other leaders permission to try. To start small. To fail safely. And build from common ground rather than from scratch.

We also contributed to broader sectoral resilience. By aligning our practices with those of other institutions, we helped shape emerging norms:

- What "good" safeguarding looks like in an AI context.
- How to evaluate agents responsibly.
- What CPD is needed for sustainable uptake.

In doing so, we didn't just scale our systems, we helped scale the movement.

Tip: Share what works. Share what doesn't. Build communities of practice.

Don't wait until everything is perfect to share your work. Others will benefit just as much from your failures and missteps as from your wins.

- Host open briefings or webinars.
- Publish toolkits or policy templates.
- Reach out to peers for input, and return the favour.
- Join sector networks, and contribute actively.

Transformation is faster when it's shared.

More importantly, it's smarter, safer, and more sustainable.

And in a field as consequential as AI in education, none of us can afford to go it alone.

Keep Asking the Right Questions

As tools mature, the questions must evolve. When AI first enters an organisation, it's natural, and often necessary, for the conversation to begin with questions of efficiency: *What can it automate? What can it improve?* But as confidence grows and capabilities expand, these early questions must give way to deeper ones:

- *What should AI do in our setting?*
- *Who is benefiting, and who is being left behind?*
- *How can we use AI to elevate equity, not just productivity?*

For us, this transition marked a pivotal moment. With the technical foundations in place, and a culture of co-creation established, we began to ask: *How can AI help us listen better?*

Not just to what students say, but to what their behaviour, engagement patterns, and support needs might be silently signalling.

This shift reframed AI not just as a time-saving tool, but as a justice-enabling one. We started to explore how agents might be used to:

- Proactively identify signs of disengagement.
- Tailor interventions for SEND students based on personalised learning pathways.
- Surface hidden barriers to access in policies or processes.
- Translate student feedback into actionable insights at scale

This was not an abstract ambition. It was a moral and operational imperative. As public institutions charged with widening participation and reducing disadvantage, we recognised that AI could, and should, play a role in amplifying student voice, not just replicating institutional norms.

In this sense, our work aligned closely with the ethics of care in education (Noddings, 2005), which emphasises attentiveness, responsiveness, and relational trust. AI, used responsibly, can help extend that attentiveness into spaces where human eyes and ears cannot always reach, surfacing early warnings, unmet needs, or inequitable outcomes.

But this only works if the intent is clear. Left to drift, AI can easily entrench the very gaps it promises to close. Algorithmic bias, inaccessible interfaces, and over-reliance on historical data can silently reinforce inequality if we are not careful. That's why the questions must evolve, not just from *Can we build it?* to *Should we?*, but from *Who benefits?* to *Who decides?*

We began to see each new agent as an opportunity to build inclusion in, not retrofit it later. Whether that meant multilingual interfaces, consent-first models for under-18s, or tools that supported neurodiverse learners with voice-to-text input, it was about using design as a lever for dignity.

Tip: Use AI to close gaps, not just streamline processes. Let your mission, not the technology, set the destination.

- Run equity audits of your AI use: Who uses it most? Who avoids it? Why?
- Invite marginalised student groups to help shape your agents.
- Prioritise tools that improve access to support, not just information.
- Train AI not only to *answer* questions, but to *surface* the questions you're not asking.

Ultimately, the power of AI in education isn't in how fast it works, it's in how wisely we use it.

It's not in the number of agents deployed, but in the gaps those agents help us close.

Efficiency matters. But equity matters more.

And when AI serves inclusion, it doesn't just scale your systems, it reinforces your values.

Don't Wait for Certainty, Lead with Courage

Nobody is going to give you permission (or not) to explore AI. There will never be a perfect moment. One of the clearest lessons from our journey, is that waiting for the stars to align, perfect policies, flawless tools, total consensus, is a recipe for inaction. The landscape of artificial intelligence is dynamic by design. Tools evolve weekly. Legislation plays catch-up. Ethical debates shift with each new breakthrough. If leaders wait for certainty, they will be left behind.

What we learned is this: you don't need certainty, you need readiness. And readiness isn't about ticking every box. It's about having a shared purpose, a strong culture of learning, and a team that trusts each other enough to walk into the unknown together.

There is wisdom in caution, but paralysis serves no one. What matters is not eliminating every risk in advance but knowing how you'll *navigate* them together. This is where the concept of *adaptive leadership* becomes essential. As Heifetz and Linsky (2002) argue, the most effective leaders in uncertain environments are those who can distinguish between technical problems (with known solutions) and adaptive challenges (which require experimentation, new learning, and cultural change). Implementing AI in education is the latter.

Courage in this context doesn't mean recklessness. It means proceeding with integrity, clarity, and a belief in the capacity of your people to learn, adapt, and lead. It means building systems that are transparent, agents that are co-designed, and guardrails that are rooted in ethics, not because you've got everything right, but because you're committed to doing things right, together.

We didn't have a master plan for everything. But we did have a culture of inquiry, where experimentation was welcomed, feedback was fast, and failure was seen as a necessary step toward better design. And that culture created momentum.

Tip: Leadership is not about having all the answers, it's about creating the conditions for others to find them.

- Set the tone by modelling curiosity, not control.
- Acknowledge what you don't know and invite others to explore it with you.
- Frame AI not as a solution, but as a *question*: How could this help us work better, fairer, smarter?
- Celebrate the small steps, each iteration, each insight, each moment of shared learning.

Ultimately, starting the AI journey is less about choosing the *perfect tool* and more about choosing the *right mindset*. A mindset that values progress over perfection. Dialogue over decree. People over process.

The world won't wait. Nor should we. But when we lead with courage, care, and a clear sense of purpose, we discover that the right time to start isn't *someday*, it's *today*.

Legal Compliance: Navigating the Regulatory Landscape

As artificial intelligence transitions from experimental projects to operational systems in educational institutions, leaders must be vigilant about the legal frameworks governing its use. Compliance is not optional, it is foundational to trust, accountability, and sustainability.

AI regulation is evolving rapidly, and laws differ significantly across jurisdictions. For education leaders operating within a specific national context, or engaging with international partners, it is vital to understand and adhere to the legal standards relevant to their country or region.

Generative AI Compliance and Safeguarding

In line with the UK Government's 2024 guidance on the use of generative AI in education, our implementation strategy was underpinned by robust safeguarding and compliance practices.

- At no point was sensitive data input into public-facing AI platforms.
- All development took place within secure tenancies, governed by GDPR-compliant policies.
- Tools used by staff or students were clearly labelled as AI-powered and signposted accordingly.
- Safeguarding protocols were embedded in agent design, with red-team testing, input/output logging, and monitoring for harmful prompts.

- Parents and students were informed of AI use via appropriate communication channels, with clear routes to raise concerns.

Understanding Your Local and Regional Legal Environment

The implementation of AI must begin with a clear understanding of applicable laws on AI, data protection, algorithmic transparency, student rights, and digital ethics. While this book draws upon the practical experience of AI adoption in a UK college setting, its readership may include professionals across Europe, North America, Asia-Pacific, and beyond. As such, the following examples highlight the diversity and scope of AI regulation globally:

- **European Union – EU AI Act**
  The EU AI Act, one of the world's first comprehensive AI regulatory frameworks, classifies AI systems by risk level and imposes obligations accordingly. High-risk systems, such as those used in education for grading, admissions, or behavioural assessment, must comply with strict transparency, documentation, and human oversight requirements. Institutions operating in or collaborating with partners in the EU must ensure their systems meet these standards.
- **United States**
  The US does not yet have a unified federal AI law, but sector-specific regulations (e.g., FERPA for student data) and state-level legislation are increasingly shaping AI governance. The White House's *Blueprint for an AI Bill of Rights* provides guiding principles for ethical AI use, including protections against algorithmic bias and the right to human alternatives.
- **United Kingdom**
  While no specific AI Act currently exists in the UK, existing legislation, such as the UK GDPR and Equality Act, applies to AI usage, particularly in relation to data

protection and discrimination. The UK Government has also published an AI Regulation White Paper, which champions a context-specific, decentralised approach to AI oversight.

- **Australia**
  Australia's approach focuses on a mix of voluntary principles and emerging regulatory reform. The Australian Human Rights Commission has also examined AI through the lens of fairness and accountability. The *AI Ethics Framework* provides guidance for responsible innovation, particularly in sectors like education and public service.

A Practical Toolkit for Compliance

To support education providers in navigating this landscape there may be tools and models available to support you, in the EU for example, Matthew Wemyss has developed a practical AI Adoption Toolkit, a resource aimed at operational leaders integrating AI into their institutions. The toolkit includes checklists, legal guidance summaries, and risk assessment templates that map regulatory requirements to the functional areas where AI is deployed.

Wemyss's work underscores a central theme of this book: leadership must stay ahead of the regulatory curve, not merely to avoid penalties, but to foster ethical innovation and uphold public trust.

Embedding Compliance into Strategic Planning

Legal compliance must not be an afterthought. It should be embedded in strategic planning, procurement, development, and staff training. Appointing a data protection officer or working closely with legal counsel may be necessary when scaling AI use. Institutions should also engage with national regulators and sector bodies to stay abreast of updates and best practices.

In an age where AI systems can automate decisions that affect people's lives, including students and staff, compliance is about more than ticking legal boxes, it is a commitment to fairness, transparency, and human dignity.

Final Thoughts: Leading with Intention, Building with Integrity

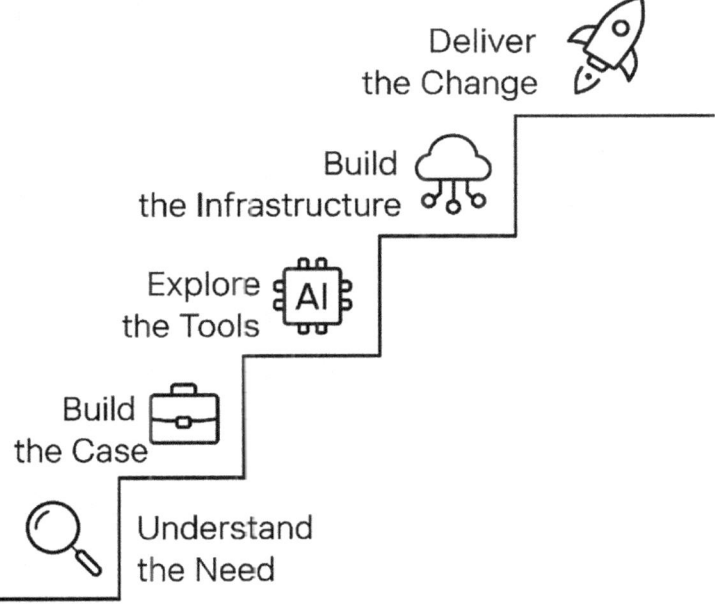

Our story of AI adoption is not one of overnight transformation or flawless execution. It is a story of thoughtful leadership, principled risk-taking, and a relentless focus on what truly matters: people.

AI did not fix our challenges. It reframed them. It didn't replace our teams. It empowered them. And while the technology was new, the values that guided us, clarity, purpose, inclusion, and trust, were not. They were the constants that enabled us to navigate the unknown with confidence and care.

What made the difference wasn't just the tools we built. It was the mindset we adopted. We didn't pursue innovation for its own sake. We asked what problems needed solving, what burdens needed easing, and what systems needed redesigning so our people could thrive.

We learned that AI can be a catalyst, but only if you build the conditions around it for meaningful, sustainable change. That means strategic alignment from the outset. It means building trust before building systems. It means designing with, not for, your teams. And above all, it means embedding your values into every line of code, every policy, and every conversation.

For other leaders embarking on this journey, the path ahead will not be identical. But the principles remain the same. Start with purpose. Build with integrity. Share what you learn. And never lose sight of who the technology is meant to serve.

Because AI isn't the future of education. People are.

And when we lead with both heart and head, when we balance ambition with ethics, and when we view change not as disruption but as opportunity, we don't just adopt technology, we shape a better future with it.

Let that be our legacy.

> **Chapter 8: What We Learned**
> - Strategy must lead technology, never the other way around.
> - Focus on people, not just products.
> - Build in phases: start small, scale smart, and own the journey.
> - Inclusion, ethics, and clarity of purpose are the real drivers of sustainable change.

- Without a clear AI policy, innovation risks becoming guesswork – set expectations early to ensure safe, confident, and values-aligned adoption.
- Know the law before you launch. Legal compliance isn't optional, it's essential. From the EU AI Act to regional data laws, every country has its own rules. Understand them, plan for them to stay on the right side of progress.

Chapter 8: 💡 Key Reflection Questions

- Have you established a clear, values-led AI policy, regardless of how far along your implementation journey is?
- Are you leading with long-term strategy rather than short-term hype when exploring AI opportunities?
- What small, low-risk pilots could you launch today to start learning and building momentum?
- Where does it make strategic sense to build your own AI solutions, and where should you buy in?
- How are you ensuring that people remain at the heart of your AI strategy, not just products and platforms?
- Are inclusion, ethics, and accessibility built into your design processes from the very beginning?
- How well are you thinking in systems, not silos, to ensure AI initiatives are connected and coherent?
- What are you doing to build internal capacity so your AI adoption can thrive and endure over time?
- How open is your institution to external perspectives, collaboration, and constructive challenge?
- Are you waiting for certainty, or are you prepared to lead with courage and a commitment to learning?

CHAPTER 9: ENOUGH ABOUT ME, WHAT ABOUT YOU?

You've read the journey. Now it's time to map your own.

You've seen what worked (and what didn't), how we started small and scaled, and how values stayed at the heart of every decision. But your context is different, and your response needs to be your own.

This chapter is your bridge from case study to action plan. It's a hands-on, practical toolkit designed to move you and your team from inspiration to implementation. Whether you're cautiously exploring or confidently experimenting, the resources here will help you:

- Reflect on where you are
- Identify where you want to go
- Structure your first (or next) steps with clarity and confidence

Each tool is built on real-world learning, and designed to support leaders, teachers, and teams across the sector. Use them to plan pilots, guide conversations, and surface risks before they become problems.

AI Agent Design Canvas

Before building anything, ground your thinking. Use this short framework with your team to scope a potential agent. It works like a business model canvas, helping you pressure-test ideas before time or money is spent.

As part of your planning, consider whether the agent will require API connectivity to internal systems (e.g., MIS, timetable platforms, finance systems). Will this be a one-way integration (read-only) or a two-way connection (read and write)? Two-way APIs introduce greater risk and require robust security measures.

Also, reflect on ethical boundaries. Could the agent hallucinate or return inaccurate information? If so, how will users be warned or protected? Transparency, audit logs, and confidence thresholds can help manage this.

It is also essential that you consider safeguarding and other risks in the development of an agent. Especially for student-facing tools (like Student Buddy or Bespoke LLM), this checklist helps ensure you've thought through the risks and designed with protection and transparency in mind:

Consider using a traffic light system:

- **Green**: Internal-only, low-risk, no sensitive data.
- **Amber**: Operational or staff-facing, with safeguards.
- **Red**: Student-facing or sensitive. Requires full governance.

Before building anything, ground your thinking. Use this one-page framework with your team to scope a potential agent. It works like a business model canvas, helping you pressure-test ideas before time or money is spent.

Section	Prompt
Problem to solve	What task are we trying to streamline or improve?
Target user	Who will use the tool? Staff, students, admin, parents?
Data source	Where will it get its information from?
Expected benefit	Will it save time, reduce errors, avoid stress?

Safeguarding/ privacy risks	Are there red flags?
"What it should never do"	What are your hard limits?
Success criteria	How will we measure impact?

Use this canvas in team meetings, hackathons, or strategic planning sessions. It prevents scope creep and anchors ideas in actual need.

AI Readiness Self-Audit (for SLTs)

This reflection tool helps you understand where your organisation is starting from, and where capacity may need to be developed:

- Do we have a clear digital strategy that includes AI readiness?
- What is our current digital estate like, is it sufficient or does it need to be improved as a priority?
- Do we have legacy systems that need to be ended or removed?
- Are staff confident using our current digital tools, and are digital skills part of ongoing CPD?
- Do we have a named AI lead or digital innovation champion with time and authority to act?
- Are we confident in our data protection and information governance practices, particularly around AI-generated content?
- Are there existing pain points or inefficiencies that AI could address in a meaningful way?
- Is our organisational culture open to experimentation, or risk-averse?
- Are we set up to evaluate AI pilots (qualitatively and quantitatively)?
- Have we considered ethical implications, hallucination risks, and how we'll manage transparency?

- Can we confidently explain to governors, parents, and staff why and how AI is being introduced?

Use this audit as a leadership team discussion starter, part of strategic planning, or an icebreaker for whole-staff CPD. Revisit it regularly to track progress.

Anatomy of an AI Project Budget

Costs are real, but manageable with clarity. Here's a breakdown of how investment is phased to allow you to understand the potential financial implications:

Phase	What It Covered	Allocated Budget	Time Frame
Discovery & Audit	Consultant time, deep dive, staff workshops		
Build & Dev	Agent design, API integration, dev support		
Training	CPD sessions, resource creation		
Infrastructure	Hosting, tenancy security, cloud credits		

Additional Considerations:

- **API Licensing or Access Fees:** Some systems (MIS, HR, finance) may charge for secure API access, especially if two-way integration is required.
- **Ongoing Maintenance and Updates:** If you're building agents in-house, budget time and cost for regular updates, retraining, and technical support.
- **Safeguarding and Audit Tools:** Consider investing in logging systems, dashboards for prompt reviews, or third-party red-teaming services.

- **Comms and Engagement:** Don't underestimate the cost (and value) of internal branding, user guides, comms campaigns, and feedback loops.

These costs aren't just financial, they're strategic investments. The return comes not just in saved hours, but in better decisions, reduced error rates, improved morale, and greater resilience.

3 Month Action Plan: A Starting Roadmap

You don't need to do everything at once. This phased roadmap reflects how you might approach your early AI implementation, it balances strategic clarity with manageable pace:

Month	Focus	Key Activities
1	Stakeholder Engagement	Share your AI vision with SLT and staff; run discovery workshops to surface hopes, fears, and ideas; appoint a named AI lead with time and responsibility; communicate clearly with governors and trustees.
2	System Audit	Map out core workflows and operational bottlenecks; identify systems that could benefit from AI support; draft AI Agent Canvases for 2–3 promising use cases; assess what systems require API integration and note the risks of one-way versus two-way connections.
3	Begin Pilot Build	Choose one low-risk agent to build (e.g. staff-facing admin tool); test extensively and run a red-teaming simulation; prepare a basic logging and monitoring framework; get user feedback and iterate based on real-world use.

Consider using this roadmap as a guide in SLT away days or digital strategy meetings. It's not about speed; it's about starting well.

Leadership Skills and CPD Reflection Tool

AI leadership isn't just about tech. It's about people, purpose, and clarity. Use the checklist below to reflect on your development needs as a leader and to guide CPD conversations across your organisation:

As a leader, can I...

- Articulate how AI aligns with our mission, strategy, and values?
- Lead a change conversation with clarity, empathy, and authority?
- Understand the risks, limitations, and ethical implications of AI (including hallucinations, bias, and data privacy)?
- Build a culture of trust, psychological safety, experimentation, and learning?
- Distinguish between opportunities to build in-house and those better served by external solutions?
- Interpret technical feedback and evaluation reports to guide iteration?
- Support and coach colleagues through digital transformation?
- Navigate the governance requirements of AI implementation (e.g. DPO compliance, procurement, audit trails)?
- Champion inclusive and accessible design in AI tools and projects?

You can use this tool as part of your personal development planning, as a reflective exercise during SLT meetings, or as the foundation for a wider leadership CPD programme. Consider revisiting it termly to track growth and uncover evolving needs.

You Now Have The Knowledge, What Will You Do With It?

The next step isn't to build the perfect AI tool. It's to take one thoughtful step, grounded in purpose, shaped by people, and framed by possibility.

These frameworks are here to guide, not constrain. Adapt them to your setting, challenge them with your team, and iterate as you learn. Use them to build alignment, spark curiosity, and reduce the fear that can come with change.

Above all, remember that AI implementation is as much about trust, ethics, and empathy as it is about data, APIs, or automation. The real impact comes not from the technology alone, but from the integrity, courage, and clarity of the people who lead it.

Let this be your call to action: not just to adopt AI, but to shape it with intention, equity, and care, for the benefit of every learner and every colleague your institution serves.

> **Chapter 9: 🎨 What We Learned**
> - AI is not one-size-fits-all. Use design canvases and audits to tailor your approach.
> - Safeguarding is everyone's responsibility. Thoughtful design can prevent harm before it occurs.
> - Start with clarity. Use structured planning, not just enthusiasm, to drive sustainable innovation.
> - Costs should reflect priorities. Budget not only for technology, but for people, training, and governance.
> - Small pilots are powerful. One good use case can create momentum for change.
> - Leadership matters. The skills to lead AI implementation aren't just technical – they're cultural, ethical, and human.
> - Reflection fuels growth. These tools aren't checklists to complete once; they're scaffolding for ongoing development.

Chapter 9: 💡 Key Reflection Questions

- Which operational challenges in your setting would benefit most from a well-designed AI agent?
- Have you clearly defined what success looks like for your first AI pilot, and how you'll measure it?
- What risks or safeguarding issues could arise from your AI use, and how will you address them from day one?
- Are your staff and students aware they're interacting with AI, and do they understand what that means?
- Where are your current limitations in digital maturity, and what steps could help close those gaps?
- What level of integration do your proposed AI tools require, and what governance is in place to manage APIs responsibly?
- How will you ensure your AI strategy remains grounded in values, not just technology?
- What skills or mindsets does your leadership team need to strengthen to lead AI transformation confidently?
- Are you budgeting for the real cost of AI implementation, including training, oversight, and iteration?
- How will you make reflection, review, and iteration an embedded part of your AI journey?

BONUS CHAPTER: OPERATIONAL EXCELLENCE AND THE ISBL FRAMEWORK

In an era where educational institutions are navigating the complexities of limited resources, technological advancements, and evolving policy landscapes, the imperative for operational transformation has never been more pressing. The Institute of School Business Leadership (ISBL) has responded to this challenge by developing the OpEx for Education framework, a sector-specific approach designed to embed continuous improvement and high-quality service at the heart of operations.

Operational Excellence, or OpEx, is more than a set of tools. It's a mindset, a philosophy that embeds continuous improvement deep within the DNA of an organisation. At its heart, it's about creating the conditions where every process, every action, and every person is aligned around one core aim: delivering greater value, more effectively, for those we serve.

In the context of education, that means streamlining the operational backbone of our institutions so that teachers can teach, students can learn, and leaders can lead, without being bogged down by inefficiencies, silos, or unnecessary complexity.

As previously mentioned, public services, especially state-funded education, face a persistent and often intensifying challenge: deliver better outcomes with fewer resources. At the same time, we're expected to serve increasingly diverse needs, respond to rapid policy shifts, and remain agile in an uncertain world. It's no wonder that systems groan under the weight of bureaucracy, disconnected working practices, and inconsistent service quality.

But this is precisely where Operational Excellence becomes not just relevant, but essential.

OpEx enables schools and colleges to move from reactive firefighting to proactive problem-solving. It offers a structured yet flexible approach to tackling issues such as:

- Fragmented workflows and long lead times
- Departmental silos and duplicated effort
- Inconsistent service quality and decision-making based on outdated data
- A culture of compliance rather than improvement

It's not a quick fix, but it does offer a playbook. And in the hands of skilled leaders and empowered teams, that playbook can transform the day-to-day experience of education delivery.

The power of OpEx lies not in grand strategy documents but in everyday actions:

- **Leaner processes** in admissions, payroll, procurement, and reporting reduce the drag on operational teams.
- **Optimised support services** ensure that information, systems, and guidance are where people need them, when they need them.
- **Standardisation**, where appropriate, makes it easier to scale what works and eliminate what doesn't.
- **Staff-driven innovation**, underpinned by root-cause analysis, puts the expertise of frontline colleagues at the centre of change.

Above all, Operational Excellence is a cultural commitment. It reframes improvement as everyone's responsibility, not the remit of a single department or initiative. It asks us to value progress over perfection and to celebrate the small wins that, over time, amount to significant transformation.

As we've seen throughout this book, the most powerful change occurs at the intersection of culture and capability. And this is where OpEx and digital innovation are truly complementary. Together, they offer the means and the mindset to reimagine how we work.

In 2023/24, the ISBL took a bold step forward. Recognising the untapped potential of OpEx in the education sector, they commissioned a major research project, drawing on expertise from both UK and US contexts, to explore how these principles could be codified for schools and trusts.

The result was *OpEx for Education*™, a sector-specific framework that captures the essence of Operational Excellence through an education lens. Built around ten domains, the framework provides a clear, practical foundation for school and trust leaders who want to improve performance with purpose.

Here's a brief look at the framework:

Domain	Focus
Impact on Teaching and Learning	Capturing the needs of school leaders and teachers, and aligning processes to deliver and measure against these expectations.
Process and Quality Control	Developing "one best way" processes that deliver right-first-time outcomes and draw on best practice and standards.
Resource Planning and Deployment	Matching resources to demand efficiently, and adapting to real-time changes without compromising service.
Data, Performance Measurement, and Action	Turning data into insight, defining KPIs, and using performance intelligence to drive decisions.

Skills and Human Performance	Identifying and developing the right skills across support teams, and managing performance proactively.
Operations Management Capability	Elevating the role of first-line managers as leaders of operational excellence, with the right training and recognition.
Operational Risk and Quality Assurance	Integrating risk management and QA to ensure robust, reliable, and safe delivery of services.
Productivity and Cost Control	Understanding value and cost, managing productivity, and ensuring procurement drives both quality and efficiency.
Technology Effectiveness	Making the most of current tech, understanding future needs, and aligning digital systems with strategic goals.
Continuous Improvement	Embedding improvement as an everyday activity – not an occasional intervention.

This framework is not a checklist. It's a conversation starter, a lens through which to view our operational environment with fresh eyes. It prompts us to ask better questions: Are we delivering value? Are we using our people and resources wisely? Are we learning and improving every day?

When combined with the digital capabilities discussed in earlier chapters, OpEx becomes a bridge, connecting strategic ambition with operational reality. It's not about doing more with less. It's about doing *better* with what we have.

And that's what this book has always been about: building a future where excellence is not just a goal, but a way of working.

KEY TERMS AND DEFINITIONS

This glossary provides definitions for key terms used throughout the book to support readers in understanding the concepts central to AI implementation and operational transformation in education.

AI Agent
A software entity built using AI technologies that automates tasks or supports decision-making in a specific domain. In the book, agents are bespoke tools designed to enhance back-office efficiency, such as the GCSE Results Agent or Student Buddy.

Application Programming Interface (API)
A set of rules and protocols that allows different software systems to communicate. APIs enable AI agents to interact with platforms like MIS, or external data sources.

Back End
The underlying systems, infrastructure, and logic that power an application but are not directly seen or interacted with by end users.

Bespoke LLM
A secure, institution-specific large language model interface built within the organisation's digital environment. Designed to ensure privacy, alignment with safeguarding protocols, and scalability without reliance on third-party platforms.

Black Box
A term used to describe a system or process, whose internal workings are not visible or understandable to the user.

Cloud Infrastructure
The collection of hardware, software, storage, and networking resources delivered over the internet that supports computing services and applications.

Cyber Essentials
A government-backed UK certification that demonstrates an organisation has key cybersecurity protections in place. It formed part of the foundational digital safety work for AI deployment in the college.

Diffusion of Innovation Theory
A model explaining how innovations are adopted, highlighting stages such as awareness, persuasion, decision, implementation, and confirmation. Referenced to guide cultural and behavioural change in AI adoption.

Digital Tenancy
The secure digital environment owned and managed by the institution, within which AI systems and agents are hosted to maintain control over data, security, and compliance.

EdTech (Education Technology)
A term used to describe the use of digital technology to support and enhance teaching, learning, and the management of educational institutions.

Edge Case
Unusual or extreme input that tests the robustness of an AI system. Edge cases were deliberately used during the "red team" testing phase to ensure tools were safe and reliable.

Enterprise Software
A large-scale application designed to support business or organisational processes. Enterprise software helps institutions manage functions such as finance, HR, operations, and customer

relations. In education, it can include operating systems and office application suites often forming the digital backbone for AI agent integration and automation.

Front End
The part of a software application that users interact with directly.

Hallucinations (AI)
A phenomenon where an AI system, particularly a language model, generates content that is factually incorrect, misleading, or entirely fabricated, despite appearing plausible.

Jisc Framework
A digital capability assessment model used to evaluate organisational digital maturity. Referenced to support decision-making around AI readiness and digital strategy.

Large Language Model (LLM)
An AI system trained on vast amounts of text to generate human-like responses. In the book, LLMs form the basis for tools like Bespoke LLM and other generative AI agents.

Management Information System (MIS)
A centralised digital platform used by educational institutions to collect, manage, and report on student, staff, and organisational data. MIS systems typically handle functions such as enrolment, attendance, timetabling, assessments, and safeguarding records.

Operational Efficiency
The strategic goal of improving processes and reducing waste, friction, or duplication in educational institutions. Central to the rationale behind implementing AI agents in back-office systems.

Prompt Engineering
The practice of crafting effective and precise inputs (prompts) to guide AI systems, particularly large language models, toward producing accurate, useful, or creative outputs.

Red Team Testing
A method of testing AI tools by challenging them with complex, inappropriate, or ambiguous inputs to identify vulnerabilities or unsafe responses before deployment.

Safeguarding-by-Design
The principle of embedding protective features within the architecture of AI tools to prevent misuse, such as restricting certain outputs or logging user interactions for oversight.

SaaS (Software as a Service)
A software delivery model in which applications are hosted by a service provider and accessed via the internet, typically through a subscription.

Sandbox Site
A secure, isolated digital environment used for testing new tools, applications, or features without impacting live systems or real data.

Smart Efficiency
A term coined in the book to describe a shift from speed-based productivity to strategic, AI-enabled working that prioritises purpose, values, and user experience.

Student Buddy
A custom-built AI agent designed to centralise and simplify student access to college services and information via natural language queries.

Technology Acceptance Model (TAM)
A behavioural model stating that perceived usefulness and ease of use influence how people adopt technology. Used to guide the implementation strategy and professional development in the AI programme.

ACKNOWLEDGEMENTS

This book is the product of more than just one voice, it is a reflection of a collective journey made possible by a community of visionary thinkers, generous collaborators, and relentless champions of innovation in education.

First and foremost, I want to thank my boss, whose strategic insight and leadership continue to shape not only my personal development but the future of our sector. Your commitment to education and guidance has been a source of motivation and inspiration.

To the rest of the Senior Leadership Team, I cannot thank you enough for your challenge, support, guidance and understanding. You have each taught me so much in a short space of time.

To **Stephen Morales**, thank you for believing in this work and for consistently advocating for the vital role of business leadership in education. Your support and encouragement have meant a great deal, both professionally and personally.

My sincere thanks to **David Foster, Lord Zine Eddine, Dan Fitzpatrick, Prof. Rose Luckin, Al Kingsley MBE** and **Matthew Wemyss,** leaders and innovators who are pushing boundaries in AI and education. Your thought leadership and wisdom has helped me challenge assumptions, broaden my thinking, and stay rooted in ethical, learner-focused practice.

To **Sir Anthony Seldon,** thank you not only for your kind endorsement but also for your pioneering spirit and tireless advocacy for meaningful, values-led change in education.

To **Julia Adamson MBE** and **Rob Robson,** your roles in shaping the national conversation on digital transformation and your support throughout this journey have been invaluable. Thank you for opening doors, making connections, and lifting others up as you go.

A special thank you to **Charlie Davis,** for your technical wisdom and practical challenge when I needed it most. Your input helped transform ambition into actionable strategy.

I cannot forget the digital artist (creative wizard) that has supported me on this venture **Ethan Thomas.**

To the team at the College, thank you for trusting in this vision, embracing change, and co-creating something truly meaningful. This book is a tribute to your courage, commitment, and capability.

Finally, to my family, my wife and two sons, you are my foundation and my inspiration. Your love, patience, and belief in me make everything possible and you always support me in "the next thing" no matter what it is, thank you.

REFERENCES

Burke, W.W. and Litwin, G.H. (1992) A causal model of organizational performance and change. *Journal of Management*, 18(3), pp. 523–545. Available at: https://doi.org/10.1177/1059601192222001 [Accessed 16 Apr. 2025].

Centre for AI Safety. (2025) *Agent governance: a field guide.* [online Available at: https://static1.squarespace.com/static/64edf8e7f2b10d716b5ba0e1/t/6801438c58c269237499 5db0/1744913293841/Agent+Governance_+A+Field+Guide.pdf [Accessed 18 Apr. 2025].

Davis, F.D. (1989) Perceived usefulness, perceived ease of use, and user acceptance of information technology. *MIS Quarterly*, 13(3), pp.319–340. Available at: https://doi.org/10.2307/249008 [Accessed 16 Apr. 2025].

Edmondson, A.C. (1999) Psychological safety and learning behavior in work teams. *Administrative Science Quarterly*, 44(2), pp.350–383. Available at: https://doi.org/10.2307/2666999 [Accessed 16 Apr. 2025].

Hiatt, J. (2006) *ADKAR: A model for change in business, government and our community.* 1st ed. Prosci Research. Available at: https://www.prosci.com/methodology/adkar [Accessed 16 Apr. 2025].

Institute of School Business Leadership (ISBL) (2019) *Professional standards for school business leaders.* ISBL. Available at: https://isbl.org.uk/professional-standards/ [Accessed 16 Apr. 2025].

Jisc (2015) *Building digital capability.* Jisc Research. Available at: https://www.jisc.ac.uk/rd/projects/building-digital-capability [Accessed 16 Apr. 2025].

Kotter, J.P. (1995) Leading change: Why transformation efforts fail. *Harvard Business Review*, 73(2), pp.59–67. Available at: https://hbr.org/1995/05/leading-change-why-transformation-efforts-fail [Accessed 16 Apr. 2025].

Lewin, K. (1947) Frontiers in group dynamics. *Human Relations*, 1(1), pp.5–41. Available at: https://libguides.reading.ac.uk/change/lewin [Accessed 16 Apr. 2025].

Morales, S. (2022) *Barriers to joined-up leadership.* Institute of School Business Leadership. Available at: https://isbl.org.uk [Accessed 16 Apr. 2025].

Rogers, E.M. (2003) *Diffusion of Innovations.* 5th ed. New York: Free Press.

Wemyss, M. (2025) *AI in Education: An EU AI Act Guide.* Independently published. Available at: https://www.amazon.com/AI-Education-EU-Act-Guide/dp/B0DWY1N3TF [Accessed 16 Apr. 2025].

www.ingramcontent.com/pod-product-compliance
Lightning Source LLC
Chambersburg PA
CBHW040303170426
43194CB00021B/2880